GW00858669

REDEMPTIVE TRAUMA
Confession of a Defrocked Priest

DAVID GIFFEN

Redemptive Trauma
Copyright © 2020 by David Giffen

All rights reserved. No part of this publication may be
reproduced, distributed, or transmitted in any form or
by any means, including photocopying, recording, or
other electronic or mechanical methods, without the prior
written permission of the author, except in the case of
brief quotations embodied in critical reviews and certain
other non-commercial uses permitted by copyright law.

Tellwell Talent
www.tellwell.ca

ISBN
978-0-2288-4218-7 (Paperback)
978-0-2288-4219-4 (eBook)

"It's all wrong. By rights we shouldn't even be here. But we are. It's like in the great stories... the ones that really mattered. Full of darkness and danger they were, and sometimes you didn't want to know the end. Because how could the end be happy? How could the world go back to the way it was when so much bad happened? But in the end, it's only a passing thing, this shadow. Even darkness must pass. A new day will come. And when the sun shines it will shine out the clearer. Those were the stories that stayed with you. That meant something. Even if you were too small to understand why."

— *J.R.R. Tolkien (edited by Peter Jackson)*

This book is dedicated to all those who don't belong.

Table of Contents

Foreword

I have been involved in the treatment of people with mental health and addiction problems, in the training of clinicians in the field, and I have helped many people recover from traumatic experiences for several decades now. I am well known to not shy away from the very challenging cases. My colleagues often ask me to help lead their friends and family members through recovery and I happily do so. One day, I received a call from a colleague whose work I value very much and who told me that one of her clients had written a book about his experience with trauma and addiction. She invited me to read it. I was much swamped with work at the time and still I accepted to read it. I am glad I did.

In *Redemptive Trauma: Confession of a Defrocked Priest*, the author David Giffen describes his journey through the aftermath of abuse, the resulting shame and unhealthy behaviours he engaged in his attempts to cope, his struggles with alcohol to numb the pain and the creation of an identity to survive.

As I read through the book, I recognized many of my clients, their struggles, distressing memories, emotions, thoughts, behaviours, the loneliness deep inside, desperate search for love and support, and the others' misunderstand of who they are and what they do. I also noted in the author the courage I have seen in many of my clients, the bravery to open up, to own his mistakes and to be authentic. As the author engaged in psychotherapy and learned to face and accept the pain and the unpleasant experiences, he climbed out of his shell and he learned to accept and value himself. By accepting his truth, he could move forward and free to be who he is.

The author's very noble career ended with and became defined by a mistake he made. Although he had contributed greatly to the life of many, he then became portrayed as a villain to be excluded, not worthy of continued positive influences. This book, which emanated from his writing as part of a therapeutic activity, has become a book that many people will find useful to reflect on their own experience as a victim, as a judge, and as an observer. People with traumatic experiences can learn that they are not alone, and they can work through their own reactions to their painful memories, let go of the shame, and learn to cope in a way that allows them to grow, forgive, and love themselves. This book can help people learn that they do not have to take on the shame that is not theirs. People who judge may find out that there are many layers underlying people's actions, and that "condemned behaviours" are often reactions to traumatic experiences and these do not define an individual. The positive contributions of the sinners can still be celebrated and the offenders themselves can still be cherished and guided though recovery instead of shunned. The observers may learn to question the labels afflicted onto others, to discover the person behind the behaviour and to give a hand to the one in need. People with very different walks of life will recognize themselves in different parts of the book.

The Redemptive Trauma, a raw authentic story filled with pain and awakening, is a reminder to not fall in the trap of defining people by a behaviour and instead to try to understand the person's situation and offer help to them and adopt patience as people walk through their own recovery journey. It is an opportunity to remind ourselves that no matter how old we are, what gender we are, what profession we practice, and where we come from, we all need and deserve to be loved and cared for. It is an opportunity to understand that vulnerability and openness are not to be equated with failure, but instead they provide an opportunity to grow. No matter how bad things are there is hope.

Christine Courbasson
Ph.D., C.Psych.

Author's Note

All of the stories in this book are true.

They are written in a manner to help the reader understand the brain and memory of someone living with post-traumatic stress injuries – often experiencing multiple realities at once. Names and identifying details of some individuals have been changed in certain circumstances. Some vignettes have been retold from previously shared opportunities.

Prologue

Confession is a sacramental practice of certain Christian denominations that seeks to lay before God the shortcomings of one's life; naming the ways our choices have disconnected us from ourselves, our community, and from God. Defrocked is an ecclesial word to describe the deprivation of a member of a religious order from the sacred office they hold. A priest is a trusted member of the clergy; a member of the community who has been set apart and ordained by a bishop into lifelong ministry.

I have made confession to a priest since I was very young. Even when it had been years since I had been to worship on Sunday, I still made my way to the confessional regularly. I credit it with any sliver of claim I might have to humility. Defrocked is a state I now find myself in – not a lay person, but no longer a priest. They don't *call* it defrocked, mind you. They jazzed it up a little more and call it *Deprivation of Ministry*. A priest, I have been since the ripe old age of twenty-six, regardless of how absurd that may have seemed to so many who'd known me.

This is my final confession, as a *defrocked* priest.

֎֎֎

The Adverse Childhood Experiences study was done by Dr. Vince Felitti at Kaiser Permanente and Dr. Robert Anda at the Centers for Disease Control in America.[1] They asked 17,500 adults about their history of exposure to what they called *adverse*

---

[1] cdc.gov/violenceprevention/acestudy/

childhood experiences (ACEs). Those include physical, emotional, or sexual abuse; physical or emotional neglect; parental mental illness, substance dependence, incarceration; parental separation or divorce; or domestic violence. For every yes, you would get a point on your ACE score. ACE scores were measured against health outcomes. Sixty-seven percent of the population had at least one ACE. And 12.6 percent, one in eight, had four or more ACEs. There is a dose-response relationship between ACEs and health outcomes: the higher your ACE score, the worse your health outcomes. If someone has an ACE score of four or more, their relative risk of chronic obstructive pulmonary disease was two and a half times that of someone with an ACE score of zero. For hepatitis, it was also two-and-a-half-times. For depression, twice that. For suicidality, it was 12 times. A person with an ACE score of seven or more had triple the lifetime risk of lung cancer and three and a half times the risk of ischemic heart disease.[2] It's no joke.

My ACE score is seven. I didn't know what that meant a few years ago. But when I learned about it, it was a like ripping off a band-aid to reveal an open surgical wound. I knew what most of the pieces of my life looked like, but before I put them in order and looked upon them as a whole through the lens of the ACE study, the puzzle hadn't made much sense to me. When you add substance abuse into the mix with someone like me, you actually get to numb the pain for a longer period of time... forget all the things you don't want to remember. But the more you use, the more you need, and the more traumatic memories push their way to the surface.

When I began the process of honest, intentional psychotherapy in 2016, I really didn't know what was going on in my head. I wouldn't have believed what the coming years would have in store

---

[2] ted.com/talks/nadine_burke_harris_how_childhood_trauma_
affects_health_across_a_lifetime/

or how upside-down my life would get. I knew my brain was hard-wired a little differently than others, and that I have a lot of more interesting stories to tell than some, but as the layers peeled back on my history –and my eyes began to burn– I couldn't help but see my reflection.

I was diagnosed with Complex Post Traumatic Stress Disorder in 2018. After a lifetime of traumatic stress injuries, slowly building, one upon another, I manifested with symptoms across the board. Many of those who suffer from PTSD know the stigma that comes with this condition, or with any mental health condition. Whether people roll their eyes at you, or won't take you seriously, or talk about you behind your back. Symptoms can range from addiction and sleep deprivation to intimacy inability, depression, anxiety, and sometimes worse (DSM-5). Initiatives in Canada, like *Bell Let's Talk Day*, are a great start, but they only really work if people are willing to listen the rest of the year. Mental health issues are often unseen, covered up, and messy. They often go unnoticed and behind the scenes for years, and they can involve drugs and alcohol and sex.

Let's be honest though, if it isn't Let's-Talk-Day, people would mostly rather just not look.

When I was in treatment in Nashville, after I broke down pretty hard, I met a soldier suffering from many of the same symptoms as me. His tales of sniper fire and carrying limbs off the battlefield made me want to go home, because I couldn't compete. But at the end of the session, once we'd both shared; he confessed to me how much shame he used to carry, because he believed himself to be weak. He said his two best friends, who'd experienced everything he had, have no symptoms and have gone back to regular life at home. He said, "That's not how this works, brother! It's not what happened to you in the end. It's how well your brain was prepared to deal with it – before you went in."

TEDMED 2014

Dr. Nadine Burke Harris
Surgeon General of California

"Imagine you're walking in the forest and you see a bear. Immediately, your hypothalamus sends a signal to your pituitary, which sends a signal to your adrenal gland that says, "Release stress hormones! Adrenaline! Cortisol!" And so, your heart starts to pound, your pupils dilate, your airways open up, and you are ready to either fight that bear or run from the bear. And that is wonderful if you're in a forest and there's a bear. But the problem is what happens when the bear comes home every night, and this system is activated over and over and over again, and it goes from being adaptive, or lifesaving, to maladaptive, or health-damaging. Children are especially sensitive to this repeated stress activation, because their brains and bodies are just developing. High doses of adversity not only affect brain structure and function, they affect the developing immune system, developing hormonal systems, and even the way our DNA is read and transcribed... We are beginning to understand how to interrupt the progression from early adversity to disease and early death, and 30 years from now, the child who has a high ACE score and whose behavioral symptoms go unrecognized, whose asthma management is not connected, and who goes on to develop high blood pressure and early heart disease or cancer will be just as anomalous as a six-month mortality from HIV/AIDS. People will look at that situation and say, 'What the heck happened there?'"

GiffontheWay Blog Post: April 2018.
Written on the day of the Toronto van attack.

He wasn't born this way. He can't have been. It keeps seeping into my mind as I watch my news feed scroll carnage and chaos in my city today. The name and the photo of the perpetrator stands still, and all I can think is, he wasn't born this way. He can't have been.

You aren't born wanting to sow anarchy and fear. You aren't born wanting to take life and limb and leave the rest to suffer. You aren't born filled with hate or violence or terror in your heart. He just can't have been.

He was made in the image and likeness and love of God. Just like me. He was born with potential and possibility and promise. Just like you. He was known in his mother's womb and cherished by our creator. No different than any of us is.

He wasn't born this way. He can't have been.

But, like us all, he was born into a broken and fractured world, just like every victim and every perpetrator. He was born with the prospect and possibility of both acts of goodness and the treachery of deceit. He was born into a corrupt and corruptible world where degraded love and systemic hate can shatter the life into which we first began.

He wasn't born this way. But this is who he became.

It pains me, perpetrator, but I pray for you on this day when you rained down terror and trepidation upon my beloved home. I pray for you because I believe it is the only way I won't become what you have today. I pray for you because so much of me wants to succumb to all the hate you make me feel inside. I pray for you because Christ says it is the only way.

May the violence end with yours. May the hate end with the blood of your victims. And may the fire that burns in our hearts be a fire desperate for the world that Jesus promised us – a world where there is no more tears, no more crying, and no more pain.

He wasn't born this way.

Cookies and Criminality

Channels 40 and above were always fuzz on my television growing up. It's not something the next generation will ever be able to relate to, I imagine, as everything is now digitized and served up the way you want it. But seriously, the number of fuzzy channels you had on your television was determined by the package to which your parents subscribed. I remember days in my childhood when I'd be willing to sit right up next to the television, watching the fuzzy channel, desperately trying to see a show I wanted to watch.

Let's not yet get into what was on those channels at 2 a.m. in my teens.

That's how my brain felt at four years old: strained, stressed. Able to view, yet unable to see. Fuzzy. I think I was a bright kid. I picked up details easily and had the ability to enter deeply into emotional relationships with people I'd just met. Strangers would often comment on it to my parents, how much older I seemed. But trying to grapple with the public and private versions of my family was like watching a fuzzy TV show. I knew my Mum was always my Mum, but I couldn't understand how she could become so sad, or angry, or volatile when no one else was around, and laughed so much and was so happy and energetic when we were around others. I never questioned if something was wrong or out of place or abnormal, because... well, why would I? When I was four years old, my mother was barely twenty-three. We had emigrated from Scotland to Canada the year after I was born, leaving behind everyone I knew. I didn't know what other families were like, or

4

what "normal" was. I just knew my life. As far as I knew, it was as normal as snow on the ground at Christmas.

I have an overcharged mind and an overactive imagination. I don't ever remember a time when I could shut it off. I tried, relentlessly. I still do. But when I was a child, it drove my parents crazy at bedtime. I would come down the stairs, again, and again and again. I'd say I had a sore head, or a sore stomach, or a sore throat, or bad dreams, or that I just wanted to see if they were okay. My Dad's response was always a one liner, "Go back and turn on your side." He would dismiss me as an attention-seeking nuisance. I'm certain he's not alone in this style or approach, but there is nothing worse than that first moment of rejection from a parent. Especially when you need love so desperately. Your breath sucks back, cold, into your lungs and your eyes get hot with tears. But no matter what emotion struck me, I would not be able to shake my brain, my thoughts, my fears. Playing out every scenario again and again in my head; trying to make sense of the world in which I lived.

Mum's solution was totally different than Dad's. She would yell and scream and lose her temper –especially when my Dad wasn't around– trying to manage life raising a *wee Scottish family* in a foreign land. She would get quite close to pulling out all of her own hair at times, *alone* too often, trying to care for two kids under three, and then three under six, all before her twenty-sixth birthday. She would spank me to try and use the "best" of her upbringing's corrective method of discipline for disobedience, but frankly, that really made no sense to me either. It wasn't that I was doing something wrong, I was simply trying to make sense of our chaos and, quite frankly, she made no sense. She'd tell me to do one thing, and then shift gears entirely. She'd yell at me for not going to bed, and then come into my room hours later wanting to chat. She was a kid! I rarely understood everything we talked about. But she would always cuddle me and say nice things, after she told me all about her life. It calmed my mind and made everything seem all better for a while, and I welcomed it with open arms.

I loved my Mum. At that age, who else did I spend that kind of time with? Dad commuted long hours by transit to a job he slaved at downtown. They both talked about how we didn't want to appear too dependent on the family of my Mum's Canadian cousins, because we needed to make it ourselves. They needed time alone, and often I was more than a handful. So eventually, the solution became that I could leave the light on in my room, and stay up doing whatever I wanted, as long as I was doing it on my own. One night, I decided, if I stayed up late enough, or if they went to bed early enough, I'd be able to at least leave my room. I had played with every toy; I'd looked at every book... I quite literally started having conversations with myself, and with my stuffed animals.

I sat by the door to my room drawing circles in the carpet. I waited and waited. The moment I heard movement in the stairwell, I turned off my light. No one checked in on me. I crept into the hallway and stood frozen because I knew how much the floor creaked. Then I turned back into my room and hid under my covers, until my eyes gave way to exhaustion. I did the same, the following night, only this time, I tested the sound of the stairs. I was sure someone was going to catch me; I might have even found joy in the test of that fear. And again, I ran back up into my room, jumped onto my bed, and took cover amidst the pillows. I don't know how many nights I did this for, but it became my standard practice. I eventually found my way into the kitchen, climbed up onto the countertop, and hid as many cookies in my shirt and pants as I could manage without leaving too many recognizable crumbs behind. I would go up to my room and gorge on as many chocolate chip cookies as I had *stashed-and-run* with.

"I can breathe!" I would think to myself. I'd feel a calm come over me, and my mind relax. I would sit in the silence and darkness, feeling just enough calm to sleep.

My Mum would ask me if I was stealing cookies almost every day, and there was no way I was copping to this crime because I knew she would lose her mind. I denied it with everything I had. I came up with excuses and stories to create misdirection. I didn't like lying about it. I simply didn't want to make things worse. I wanted her to be more like the person she was when everyone else was around. I wanted to avoid the chaos I knew would come. So, I lied through my teeth.

She eventually brought my Dad into it. He didn't believe her. He said that it couldn't possibly be me, I was just a little kid. Deep down, I'm pretty sure he was insinuating that she must have lost count of how many cookies she'd had that week. This didn't help. She knew it was me, she must have. When my father asked me, I'd lie to him as well. The weight of guilt for this heavy burden on my shoulders, it actually *hurt*. But I would keep waiting up. I would keep sneaking out of my room. And I would keep lulling myself to serenity with sugar and crumbs.

At least, until I got caught. One night, when I was climbing back up the stairs in the wee hours of the night, my Mum suddenly appeared at the top. She grabbed my arm and I felt the cookies crack. She pushed me against the bed and said, "I can't believe it, you little thief. My son is a thief. Do you know what they do to thieves, David? They put them in jail. You're going to end up in jail!" She wasn't screaming, I'm almost certain of it, and my Mum sure ain't copping to that exact quote. But that's what my *fuzzy* little brain heard through my childhood ears. Words that would cut deep into the fabric of my soul, instead of bouncing off like it does for so many others.

She tucked me in, and out of a deep shame and an overwhelming fear, I stopped stealing cookies after that.

I'm an asthmatic. When I was a child, I needed puffers multiple times a day, and even an oxygen mask at times. Ventolin, for those of you haven't taken it, is a powerful steroid. In increased doses, it can create a stoned feeling for a short period of time, numbing the mind. Within days of ending the late-night thievery, I discovered my puffers on a shelf in my room, and it didn't require much work for me to climb to retrieve them. I still remember quite vividly the first time I took fifteen puffs and felt the anxiety wash away. I was not suffering, I was not afraid, I was not worried or anxious or living in fear.

I could sleep.

***

Holidays were something my parents desperately wanted to get right. I always thought it was strange the way they'd go all out with over-the-top gestures and presents and food at Christmas and Thanksgiving celebrations. It's probably only notable because it was so different from the way we functioned most of the time. My mother, who barely had enough energy to make dinner most nights of the week, wanted to cook more assorted food than we could ever hope to consume. My Dad always wanted to suck all the marrow out of the moment, trying to show us how awesome he was, by being the most fun adult we knew on those days. My parents would often argue amongst themselves on a Thanksgiving walk, or in the Christmas kitchen, but holidays were actually the closest I ever got to "normal" when I was growing up.

My parents split up when I was in my first year of university. My Mum actually drove up to my residence to surprise me with the news the night before I came home for Christmas. I think they hated each other at this point, but they so desperately still wanted to save face. My Mum was a Pastoral Associate at our local Catholic Church, having struggled to maintain consistent work due to continuous diagnosis and misdiagnosis of chronic degenerative illnesses. My Dad was an up-and-coming director of a number of technology companies on the rise and was well positioned to continue to rise himself. They had three kids, one not yet in high school, and we had perfected the art of presenting well. On some level, I believe they were trying to do what they thought what was expected and right.

The first Christmas morning after the separation was a disaster. I started to cry, and my Dad got really angry and asked me to leave the room. My mother kept trying to fix everything, from the tree trim to appetizers to scrubbing the corner underneath the sink – *anything* to not have to be in the room. As the day went on, my Dad got more intoxicated and my mother got up in his face. I don't remember what they said to each other –frankly, I was secretly drinking as well– but like I said, I'm pretty sure they had come to hate each other by this point. Dinner devolved like a typical family dinner would, and not like festive holidays in years past. There was no "Sunday best" or intentionality of discourse the way there had been in years gone by; just unspoken rage, visceral hurt, confusion and fear in the minds of my sisters and me. I left. I decided I couldn't handle it any longer. I wasn't going to fake cozying up to watch a Christmas movie while my Mum seethed and my father fell asleep, boozed out. I went out, had a few drinks myself, and crashed elsewhere before heading to work the next morning.

I was a complicated young man, but not a bad one, I don't think. I liked to party and to stay out too late and have a good time. But, if I lost control, if I drank too much, I'd often get myself entangled in an altercation with a guy who was much bigger than me. It seems hard to imagine now, that I could be both of these people. But I was an empathetic, poetry writing, fall-in-love-on-the-first-date romantic, who bled pretty badly when a wound got opened up. I was angry and vulnerable; wise, and yet so immature. I knew myself as well as I do now in some ways, but in others, I didn't have a clue.

I worked at the golf shop –my Christmas break job— until 8 o'clock on Boxing Day and I accepted an invitation to a family Christmas party at the uncle of my housemate, Sheldon. I grew up believing that Sheldon's family and mine were very different because of social class; I genuinely didn't realize that rich didn't mean healthy or successful, and poor didn't mean lazy or criminal. I thought my family had to be one thing, because my Dad's financial success made us a cut above others, and that's what he wanted me to think.

I arrived at the party with my own bottle of alcohol, a 26-ounce bottle of vodka, fresh from the liquor store. I don't remember the label or the country of origin, but I do remember thinking it would probably be *enough*. The party was incredible; people of all ages and walks of life. Children running around, men and women drinking and exchanging presents. Tipsy guys making flirtatious comments to their wives and people handing out food everywhere. I'd had a good half the bottle by the time we hit eleven, when I entered into a deep conversation with Sheldon's uncle, his father's best friend.

"You really love Sheldon like a son, don't you Leo?" I said.

"I'd give my life for that boy," he replied.

It should have been a lovely moment, recognizing how fortunate my friend was, but I had to excuse myself and went to the bathroom. I looked into the mirror and gazed at my bloodshot eyes and felt an overwhelming hatred for who I was and where I came from. I wanted a different life. I wanted to know love the way *these people* had it. I wanted more than just chaos and emptiness and preparing for the other shoe to drop. I brought the bottle into the bathroom with me and I finished every last ounce, and suddenly the pain went away. I walked back into the family room and said something funny; everyone doubled over in hysterics.

It wasn't long before I ran out of steam. In fact, people at the party said I began to hallucinate. I started confusing family members and asking questions that didn't make sense, and since I was a semi-responsible person at the time – I didn't bring my car with me— someone put me in a cab. I was sent to sleep it off at home. Now this next part, I'm only going on the evidence and facts I know to be true, because I don't have a single memory for the next series of scenes. I can't even begin to describe how much painstaking work I've done to try and retrieve the memories of that night, but it's a true blackout. I don't believe I ever will remember. When Sheldon arrived home, I was apoplectic; I was screaming, and throwing things, while calling him all sorts of names. He was my best friend and my housemate, and even someone who I thought of as a brother, but he'd had enough of my bullshit for one night, so he went into his room and locked the door. I threw the vacuum cleaner against it and he screamed at me to stop, so I went downstairs, got the keys to my Jeep, and got in.

To this day, for the life of me, I will never know how I made one turn, blew five stop signs, and drove in a residential neighbourhood without a single person coming to harm, but when a ninety degree turn in the road hit, I barrelled through someone's front yard at a hundred kilometres an hour, and straight into their home.

This next part I do remember. Being trapped amongst air bags, and bricks and shattered glass. Hearing the muffled noises of people trying to help me get out. I walked away without a scratch, miraculously, and actually recall the moment the residents phoned the police. I was handcuffed, and put in the back of a squad car, and waited for what felt like both a second and an eternity. My mother and sister arrived on the scene and my mother pressed up against the glass of the car. "What have you done?!" she said, and all I could hear was, "Criminal!" I closed my eyes and didn't open them again until I was being given a breathalyser at the police station.

I later learned that my Dad couldn't come home because he was fall-down-drunk at the cottage, and the police told me my mother said she wasn't bringing me home until I had spent the night in jail. So, the next memory I have —one of the most vivid of my life— is waking up on a metal slab in a tiny cell, behind bars. I didn't know where I was, or exactly what I'd done, or if I'd hurt someone. I was covered in puke and piss and smelled like excrement, but then I heard a voice calling my name. I closed my eyes and opened them a number of times, feeling like this was all a bad dream. But then, there was what felt like the touch of a hand on my shoulder and what can only be described as an embrace. I recognized the familiar voice as someone I knew as Jesus, telling me that he would never leave me – that no matter how far I'd fallen, or how unloved I felt, God would always be there.

I heard the words, as clear as a cottage day, "Your story's not done."

Washed in the Water

Everyone always says it's not possible I remember this, but I loved becoming a big brother. I had just turned two. It's not like I remember the moment or the event or the exact experience, but I remember coming to a deep knowledge that I wasn't the only kid anymore, and I knew this proud responsibility for *my* little sister who had just been born. I would introduce her as *my best friend* to everyone we'd meet, and as she grew, we'd spend hours playing and talking –even before she could— as we learned the kind of friendship that is usually only found in a sibling.

We shared stories, and thoughts and fears with each other. At one point we even shared a bedroom and named all our stuffed animals the most interesting names: *The Pee Man*, a blue elephant we still have somewhere. We'd stay up way past our bedtime and make up games and ask each other 20 Questions, as long as our parents didn't see or hear. As alone as I felt in so many periods of my life; when Effie was just starting to talk, and we were *thick-as-thieves*, I didn't feel like I was stuck on an island, or out on a limb.

Having watched my son Rory grow up over these last few years, I've come to recognize the importance of routine, especially at the end of his day. Every kid is different, but when he was really young, Rory loved to take that time to play quietly; to be fair, the more bubbles, the less quiet. He would think deeply and relax his muscles and really dialogue with his mom and me; it was a departure from his active, hyper, non-stop nature throughout the day. I've noticed what a difference it makes to bedtime if he slows down for a good long bath, takes his foot off the gas for a just a moment, and allows his mind to get ready to sleep.

Bath time never really had this kind of culture in my childhood family. The lack of bedtime routine was really quite fun and exciting growing up, but like many things, it was also chaotic and badly supervised. It was no holds barred, really. Running around the house naked (flash forward to my undergraduate years); getting in and out of the bath; singing songs and playing games with licence to be over-the-top and unpredictable.

When my Mum was able, she led us in a lot of crazy fun.

Like any two young siblings, Effie and I would play and argue, fight and make up. We'd go trick-or-treating together and sometimes I'd walk her to a friend's house or home from school. But like a lot of families with small children, in our house, bath-time was often communal. My Mum would get my sister and me stripped down, with a toy or two, sometimes some bubbles, and leave us to splash and play. Effie would get really mad sometimes because I was bigger and stronger and would splash her repeatedly without her being able to catch her breath. I'd hear my Mum yell from the other room, "Stop splashing your sister!" Sometimes, I would.

One night, after what seemed to be a long day, my Mum had enough. She yelled for us to get out of our clothes and into the bath immediately. She angrily washed each of us trying to get this chore done quickly –which was not something she usually did– and I still remember the strange glance from my sister, wanting to know what was wrong with Mum. I splashed Effie to be lighthearted and my Mum just yelled, "Stop!" Effie's eyes filled with tears. My Mum comforted her, and then left the room to get us towels. I calmed Effie down and we started to splash again, and we both got out of the bath together. Someone pushed someone, and she grabbed my penis as a joke, as my Mum stood at the entrance by the bathroom door.

She screamed at me. "Did you like that?" I shrank and felt incredibly small. I didn't know what to say. I was embarrassed, and ashamed and fearful for what would happen next. I wasn't sure exactly what I'd done wrong, but holy crap, it seemed to make her mad. "You can't let her do that, David!" she screamed.

She looked at me with what seemed like disgust and sent me to my room.

***

It struck me across the face like a warm wave of summer water at the beach. Refreshing, renewing, calling me to respond. Heather and I became Anglicans together after dating for six months and getting engaged. We stood before the Bishop and renewed our baptismal vows while holding hands. Heather had come from fundamentalist evangelical background and me from a Roman Catholic one. Heather having signed abstinence pledges at her youth group throughout her teens, and me having spent far too much intoxicated time in the bedroom company of far too many companions at too young an age. Heather was beautiful and normal and faithful – she was what I wanted to be. Uncomplicated. No drama. Simple – in the very best way. Someone who would give her shirt off her back to a homeless man, and still find a way to look stylish five minutes later.

To be honest, standing next to her, I felt like I was covered in shit most of the time.

I actually remember the moment, standing on the steps of St John's Chapel as the asperges water struck across my face. "I don't have to be him anymore!" I thought to myself. Everything I'd done wrong, every sin I'd committed, every sexual encounter, every personal failing; no one would have to be the wiser. I could just start again. On a superficial level, I believe this theology still. I really do and did. I am convinced –because I have seen it with my own eyes— that we can find new life in Christ and know God's love in ways that *do* transform. But my problem was, I thought that meant deeply repressing, and ferociously hiding, everything about who I was and where I came from… my formative, traumatic, and abusive history… I put so much of it in a closet. I kept it, even from Heather and, on some level, from myself.

Heather and I became physically intimate after just a few dates, which led to a few months of fun experimentation before we got engaged. She was 22 and I was 24. We fell in love and explored each other the way young couples do in those early romantic days. But after our engagement, not long after moving in, Heather started noticing some changes in me. I was no longer able to sustain the persona I held up with everyone around me in short bursts, because she was around me all of the time. She'd never really see me lose it, break down, or fall apart –except when I was drinking– and I was so ashamed of how broken I was deep inside. I came to believe she couldn't love me if she really knew. So, I would have dark days and I would have light ones. I would try and find time to recharge without her so that I could be who she needed me to be when I was with her.

It was okay. It really was at first. Things had shifted. But things shift for all couples over time. Sex began to be infrequent, but we both seemed to accept that. The truth is, we were never able to share emotional and vulnerable intimacy about who I really was, and so we were never able to build the bond necessary for long-term intimacy. She tried. I really believe she did. But I was working so hard just to survive. My brain was imploding from all the pretense and posturing, not to mention the chaos and ongoing family trauma in my life. Eventually, I was just grateful if she didn't hate me at the end of the day, never mind come to love me for me.

At some point, I think I actually stopped believing there was a "real me" anyways.

Looking back, there's no getting around it, I heard way too much about sex growing up. Now, I'm all for healthy, age appropriate sex education for children. Heck, at one point, Rory wanted to have "penis and vagina" conversations almost every day. I don't object.

But seeing literature –at the faith community of your mother's employ where you do your homework multiple times a week— hearing about sex being deviant and rooted in evil desire, masturbation being deeply sinful and pornography the spawn of Satan to corrupt the minds of weaker men. There is very little argument that Roman Catholic children of my generation were not highly sexualized.

I was in grade one when my Mum explained how she got pregnant in the early months after she began to date my Dad, and how they had to get married before I was born. She referred to it as our family's little secret, and that I was so special, I could be told it too. So, you can only imagine the hell there was to pay when I stuck up my hand in my Roman Catholic grade school class, that Christmas, to share that I was just like the baby Jesus, because my Mum was pregnant before she was married too.

Even today, having dug deep to understand and process the impact of childhood trauma in my life, I still struggle with the cross entanglement of sex and intimacy and relationships and where it all lands going forward. I've recognized how few real friends I had for a significant period of my life –for the same reason my marriage failed– an inability to be vulnerable enough to share actual honest intimacy with another human being.

It seems to me that we stand on the precipice of a reckoning, when the LGBTQ community will not stand alone in calling the Church to account for its teaching on sexuality, demanding we recognize the actual real-life consequences of the sexual teaching of the Church. Called out to recognize what happens when we force feed children a particular diet on this topic. Like much generational abuse and inherited trauma, the domino fall from generations long past is still crashing into new pieces. I love the Church; I don't ever remember a time when I didn't. From the babies I've baptized in water to the broken-down sex addict who dragged himself across the threshold of my office in tears. I love the Church. But we have to look inwards and ask what kind of damage we do to the vulnerable and developing mind when we don't engage our suffering and struggle with the truth.

The Gospel –a radical proclamation that subverted an oppressive empire seeking to subjugate, a call to freedom for prisoners and captives, a warning to powers and principalities, and an invitation for the marginalized to be given the honoured places at the table. Well, it seems to me, it has been either been tamed or weaponized in too many cases. For Christians, the Gospel is meant to be the truth; that God loved us so much, he'd take on the fragile form of a human being –and die a tragic death— so that we would know the depth of his love.

One of the great misconceptions I hear about Christianity from my non-Christian friends is that baptism is simply a solid *fire insurance* policy. As I heard from too many parents throughout my decade as a parish priest, "Grandma says if we don't do this and something happens to Georgie, he'll burn in hell!" It's not that the Church has departed from this entirely, but we are also made holy in baptism, adopted by God as brothers and sisters to each another, and anointed with God's Spirit. We are meant to be redeemed by a God who knows even our deepest wounds and skeletons and pulls us out of the water anyways.

In the spring of her birth, I had the honour of sprinkling water over the head of Effie's beautiful daughter, telling her she was Christ's beloved forever. I preached about the kind of love God had for her, for our family, and for our community; and the ways this little niece of mine had stolen my heart. I washed her with the same baptismal waters that have called so many of the broken home. Heather held her as godmother, and my sister and her husband stood grateful and full of love. I proclaimed the triumph of the Holy Spirit –washed in water and made new in love– a beautiful child of God.

"*If the Gospel is where we find healing from the harm done to us by the messages of the church, then it must also be where we find freedom. Meaning that even if it is the last thing I want to do, I absolutely have to believe the Gospel is powerful enough, transgressive enough, beautiful enough to heal not only the ones who have been hurt but also those who have done the hurting.*"

— *Rev. Nadia Bolz-Weber,*
Shameless: A Sexual Reformation

Kinky?

"I'm not my father's son.
I'm not the image of what he dreamed of
With the strength of Sparta and the patience of Job
Still couldn't be the one
To echo what he'd done
And mirror what was not in me."

—Kinky Boots

I hadn't cried in years when I turned thirty-four.

I didn't lack things to cry about or have some rare affliction with my tear ducts. I was burying the dead a couple of times a month, and I listened to stories of abuse and rape and neglect on a regular basis. But, over time, I had adapted to anesthetize myself just enough so I wouldn't even have to dig my keys into my pockets anymore to feign stigmata. It wasn't that I didn't feel anything. I had simply spent a lifetime learning all the reasons why allowing myself to feel that deeply only brought about pain. I had been life-conditioned in the knowledge that emotional reactions only brought about chaos. So, I learned ways to cope with the pain and the chaos. I learned to find ways to pretend it wasn't really there. I learned ways to divert, revert, and subvert so I'd never really have to face what had been stalking me my whole life.

A few years ago, I splurged on a Mirvish subscription –Toronto's epic Broadway— even though it was a bit beyond my budget. I had always loved the theatre growing up – improv, comedy, drama, it didn't matter. I loved putting on a costume and playing a role. It wasn't something I continued with –on stage— past the age of sixteen. So, in an attempt to claim just a little piece of the old me, I splurged. I hadn't heard much about Kinky Boots when our tickets arrived; I'd known Cindi Lauper wrote the music, that it was supposed to be incredibly funny, and the drag might blow the minds of some unsuspecting grandparents in the crowd. However, I was completely unprepared for the ways it would reach into the depths of me and squeeze out tears that I hadn't expected to find there. At the end of the first act of Kinky Boots, Simon –a beautiful, black, *bona fide* drag queen– began to sing about the ways in which he could never live up to, and into, the world his father expected. Even if he'd had the strength of Sparta and the patience of Job, he'd still never have been able to recognize him, as the beautiful ballad goes, "The best part of me is what he wouldn't see."

It was embarrassing in that theatre. I really was genuinely unprepared. People kept looking at me. My breath became uneasy and my heart started to pound, and then all of a sudden, I wasn't just welling up, there were actual full-blown tears streaming down my face. "What the fuck?" I thought to myself. I hadn't shed a single tear in four years. Now THIS?! *This* is what unblocks the ducts? I chalked it up to life as a new father, because, really, how was I to relate? Six-inch heels and more makeup than I'd ever seen before – that wasn't me. It was amazing. It was art. But me?

I often wonder if that moment wasn't the beginning of an examined awakening in my life. This strange moment in time, when I couldn't understand why I was weeping, or how it was possible I couldn't control myself; at the theatre, watching a musical about men dressing up in leather and lace.

***

One of my earliest childhood memories is my Mum telling me
I shouldn't be in anything like my Dad. Not in corporate business,
not in relationships, and certainly not as a man. She would tell me
I was an artist, and not like other boys. She'd say I was often more
feminine than masculine, and that was okay... but that my Dad
would likely never accept such *predispositions*.

When I was in my preteens, people began to notice signs
of mental unhealth in me. I would struggle to sit still, or sleep
in my bed, or keep my emotions regulated –both in joy and
despair— and so my Mum decided it was time for me to get me
some help. My Dad didn't take to this idea, as though somehow
not acknowledging the developing afflictions would make them
eventually go away. With his lack of engagement, approval or
assistance, my Mum was left in charge of addressing my mental
health.

My mother is deeply complicated. Those who know her at her
best know there is no one more compassionate or empathetic. But
at her worst, my Mum was downright scary. Formed in the bowels
of the Roman Catholic Church in Scotland, and without the
support of her husband, she would struggle to find me help. She
would take me to crackpot quasi-church therapists, who she would
encourage to help me see I was "not normal". Both my mother and
the therapists suggested I was gay, even though homosexuality was
never something I expressed.

Listen. I'm a big fan of the gays. Enough of them seem to
say it's okay for me to say it, so I'm going to go out on a limb
here: I *love* the Gays. But the gays and the Church – they have a
past filled with cruelty and marginalization. It's the reason I was
constantly surrounded by gay staff and parishioners during my
life in ministry. Regardless of the overplayed stereotype, *I was* the
straight male relationship that many of them craved in their lives;
affirmation and love from a religious father-figure, no less. I fought
a number of battles to seek the legitimization of LGBTQ clergy. I
presided at the blessing of the union between the first openly gay

Anglican bishop in Canada and his husband. I championed the overturning of the refused licensure of a gay married Deacon from California who wanted to serve in my parish.

I say this not to somehow legitimize myself with the gay community or earn more liberal street cred, as much as to say, I've had lots of time to wrestle with my own sexuality over the years. Not a tonne of safe space to do so, mind you, as a man who was engaged by twenty-four and ordained an Anglican priest by twenty-six, and raised in, well, *my* home. But I'm not gay. I just like gay people. They know suffering. They know marginalization. They know love, and often they know God. In ways a lot of straight people just don't.

At my first Pride parade in Toronto, I stepped out onto Bloor Street wearing a clergy collar and rainbow stole. No one knew my sexuality, and it really couldn't have mattered less. People thanked me for standing with them. They asked me if I was a real priest. People told me that my presence there made them feel more like one of God's people than ever before. I got to be a real redemptive symbol, which as a priest, you'd think I'd have had my fill. It was a proud, transformative, and corrective experience – I just don't think many would have realized how much it was so for *me*.

For the most part, I like women. Actually, I prefer them to men entirely. Intellectually, sexually; in humour and in companionship. But I've also been sexual with men. I currently live in an all-male household, and most of my close friends are men; some gay, some straight, some it's hard to say. I'd say on the sexual spectrum, I'm pretty straight, but that doesn't mean I don't enjoy a night of being *Queer*. I still remember the first time I heard Dennis Rodman proclaim that in his book, *Bad as I Wanna Be*. It made sense to me, even though I was only sixteen in the suburbs, and he was rebounding for Jordan and Pippen by day, while dressed in drag in New York and LA at night. But I got it. Sexuality is a messed-up concept for many of us raised with religious shame.

Being able to be as *bad as I wanna be*, makes a lot of sense for those of us who were told what we wanted just made us bad.

***

Here's the deal: I was raised by a devoutly Roman Catholic teenage girl from Scotland, living during a time of religious tension between Protestants and the Roman Catholic minority. Pregnant, in the early months of dating a Protestant man from the wrong town, she was left with very few options. By nineteen she was a teenage mother; by twenty, an immigrant in a foreign land. No significant education, few support systems and, although my Dad knew how to work like a dog, he was a workaholic and an alcoholic and didn't seem very fond of her. Mum came with a history of illness, and then she was a mother of three by twenty-five. She wanted to go home to Scotland. He didn't. She wanted to take the kids, but she had no means to survive. He wanted to take the kids, but he didn't know what to do with her. Eventually, shit would just come apart at the seams.

Frankly —on some level— their wanting to teach sex as something to run from until you're thirty-five was something they came by honestly. But let's be honest. Most of the sexual teaching of the Church is a bunch of bullshit. It's a means of control. Mostly by religious men upon women, who, throughout history and across the globe, have often stay forcibly married to, and "servicing" their husbands, because they don't have enough freedom to choose.

I will not raise Rory with the sexual teaching of the Church – progressive or conservative. I may borrow from it occasionally, as there is much beauty to be found in the ritual and theology of marriage and companionship. But there is so much muck in the mess of it, as so many women and sexual minorities have come to know in Christian Life.

I'll teach Rory three important things: Overwhelming consent, mutuality of pleasure, and safety, no matter the context.

If he can care for his partner by always ensuring actions are a choice, that both are enjoying their choice, and that both are using the best and smartest precautions for safety, then I have to hope I will have raised a young man who will always honour whatever partner chooses him.

Kinky? Damn right I am. Deal with it.

Lie to Survive

I am a terrible student. I'm not dumb or slow or learning disabled, at least not formally. But for a kid with the communication skills and charisma that I had, it's surprising to most that "A's" were not achievements I sought out. At every grade level from parent-teacher interviews at St Joseph's Catholic Elementary School in Markham to meetings with my academic advisor at Huron University College, I was accused of trying to thumb my nose at the system. Teachers would say that I was far too aware of my ability to just get by; that a phoned-in seventy-five average could be something so much more if, and I'll use the French, I just gave a shit. It was almost an art trying to keep my grades as a solid 'B', and by a certain age, I'd also enjoy how much it pissed off my Dad – especially when he was footing the bill.

I couldn't have articulated it at the time, but I always thought he was ashamed of me because I wasn't as smart as he was; because my gifts were in such different areas. Later I'd realize he was actually terrified that one day *I'd wake up* and realize how much more gifted I was than him. My Dad knows how to make money in one very particular way. But, because of how poor he grew up, because of how much he idolized money in his formative years, he equates his economic windfall with some kind of inherent brilliance. It's the American Dream (in Canada)!

Like many men of his generation –for whom I had the honour to pastor and preach and hear their confessions – he was never able to see how much my Mum coached him in his early years, or how much the colour of his skin benefited him at every opportunity given, or how lucky he got at one very particular moment in time when he worked for the right company. My father worked his ass off; I barely saw him for years. But there were those of us who sacrificed for his success, and whenever he pointed out how much smarter he was than me at my age, I just figured: Why give a shit?

At one point, in my last year of high school, I had a little fun with it. I actually bet my best female friend that if she –a consistent A+ student– wrote my final paper for me and put my name on it, *we* would never get *her* grade. *We* got a 78. I had perfected the art of the B student so well, my teachers just accepted I would never actually try. B+ on a good day.

But when I was fourteen years old, headed into grade nine, I faced my first high school exams. I felt much less confident in my ability to *wing it* for a 'B,' with my ability to charm and verbally communicate taken off the table. I studied… I really started to get into it. I even got my girlfriend at the time to quiz me the night before the first one. Standardized exams were never my strong suit, but there was no subjectivity in the marking. You got what got and you got it because you deserved it, more than not. It was a grade nine math exam. You can only imagine how motivated someone like me is to do sums. But I dug in. I learned more math in preparation than I had ever learned before, and I got a solid 82. I knew it the moment I put the pencil down, leaving the gymnasium that lunch hour, how well I'd done.

I walked home, and through the mud room door of one of my many childhood homes and heard my Mum scream at my Dad. It didn't faze me. My Mum yelling was not an uncommon occurrence in my home, and seeing my Dad dart out the front door wasn't all that weird either, because frankly I didn't expect him to be home. I went to get a Coke out of the 'fridge, and then to relax on the couch and call my girlfriend; tell her how amazing I'd done. We weren't two sentences into the conversation when I heard the first crash and then a second. I dropped the phone and ran into the next room in full view of the kitchen. There were broken plates on the floor. I saw my Mum throw a glass, and I yelled at her to stop, but it was as though she couldn't see me there. She threw one more and it almost hit me. I ran back into the next room to call my Dad and tell him he needed to get home. He could hear my tears, I'm sure of it, because he hung up immediately and must have made a U-turn. My Mum got into her car and began to open the garage door to leave. I chased her from the mud room and slammed the button on the wall to close the door. I was terrified that she'd never come back, or that she'd kill herself or someone else in such a state. She screamed at me, and I heard my Dad come up from behind and say, "Let her go." I went up the stairs and into my room and collapsed on the floor with tears and frustration and horror.

Eventually, I heard my sisters come home from school and assumed my Dad had cleaned up the mess. Later he'd return with my Mum in tow and take her up to their room and put her to bed, from wherever she'd been. Just before I fell asleep that night, he came into my room to tell me a common refrain, "Everything is good now. Let's just forget this happened and move on, and..." (like he said too many times throughout my life) "... don't tell anyone."

***

In the year before my breakdown, I would lie to Heather almost every day – about how I was feeling and what I was thinking, and eventually what I was doing. Our marriage was complicated, way before this, but fracturing my ankle the day before her 35th birthday really marked the end. I would spend most of the next four months on Hydromorphone, Morphine and Oxycodone, followed by another year attempting to quit Oxy, by using high resin cannabis products often used for cancer patients. I was not a good person during this part of my life. I was secretive and scared and paranoid. I was irritable and couldn't sleep. But four days after reconstructive surgery, on an ankle fractured in three places, completely addicted to drugs, I began my final placement as a parish priest. I was a shitty father while I was there, and a bad husband to boot, and I really only cared about how much pain *I was in*, and how I would get through the next day. I still tried to manage 60-plus-hour work weeks, even before my leg was in weight bearing shape. And as nice as everyone was to me at first – the meals that were prepared and delivered, and the calls and cards that were sent – nobody seemed to mind that I was spiraling. Not that I would have stopped, mind you, because in all honesty, I knew how badly it would all unravel if I did.

Throughout every chapter of my life, I continuously learned how to be a great liar and hide the truth of my "perfect family" as I grew up. I didn't talk about the suicide threats, or the alcoholic meltdowns or the reason family members were always estranged. I picked up *family life* right where I left off, when I married a beautiful twenty-two-year-old, who seemed so taken by everything I said. I credit Heather with any perceived clean reputation as the young golden boy priest. She was always glam and happiness, while I was in a private struggle to stay clean. I had a lot of issues that had been public in another world. But this new life with her as an Anglican seemed to wipe the slate clean.

There has always been a part of me that so desperately wanted to be loved, I would become whatever people needed to love me. The son who would fly across continents to bring his sick father home, or drive through the middle of the night to meet his mother in a hospital ward. The priest who'd seek out the dying parish – proclaiming he would turn it around. I had learned that if I took on the hardest jobs, and if I achieved what others couldn't achieve, then no one would ever ask questions about my success *or my struggles*, my blessings *or my demons*.

Live a bifurcated life long enough and you'll see the cracks begin to show. Panic attacks, insomnia, and compromised decision making, even before the ankle fracture and the drug abuse entered in. I was a complete mess for years while serving as a priest; acting out in self harm and projecting perfection and charm. Some days I even managed to convince myself.

It's why those who have to closet, must learn to lie. Again, and again and again.

***

It might have been the most consequential phone call of my entire life. Having served as the chaplain and chief advisor to my boss, friend, and area bishop, Kevin, during the 2018 episcopal election to determine the next chief Bishop for the Diocese of Toronto, the first openly gay bishop I'd ever known returned my phone call on a Tuesday morning after the long weekend. We had met at a Starbucks just the week prior to discuss my deteriorating mental health and the end of my marriage to Heather. He was supportive and loving and promised me ongoing care during this difficult time. Then, he sent me back to work.

I knew I hadn't told him everything in that moment, and I justified this by saying to myself that he couldn't possibly want to know everything. As my Bishop –in spite of our friendship– he was in serious jeopardy if I told him the rest. But after a week of drug use and self-loathing, I needed someone to know "the truth". I began to cry on the phone. I told him how I had inadvertently found myself having an emotional affair with a member of my staff that I was in love with. I told him that I had been so lonely for so long, and she was such a good friend, and that we had begun to discuss what it would look like to be together. I told him how we had a plan. I told him how she had announced her resignation already and she had another job lined up. I made the case to him that I could manage it all, that it wasn't yet out of control. Then, he sent me back to work.

I remember feeling incredibly relieved when I put the phone down; as though it would all be okay. He understood. The man had closeted his sexuality for such a significant portion of his life and knew better than most how to navigate church authority. Having disobeyed our senior bishop in the lead-up to his own election, my role offering a priestly blessing to him and his eventual husband –eight days after he was elected– was an act of damage control to ensure more conservative bishops in the country could not cry foul at this unmarried man living with another, raising two children, in defiance of his bishop. I lost a lot of friends when I played this role for Kevin, and I believed –deeply– that he would protect me during this time of chaos in *my* life. However, I would no longer think twice about sleeping with her, after we spoke.

Kevin would arrange for us to meet with the Archbishop; coaching me to focus on the dissolution of my marriage, refer to the new relationship as nothing more than a friendship, and hopefully, save all our skins. I did it. Masterfully. I think the old man almost shed a tear at one point. Kevin sat in the corner of the room and didn't say very much. I wondered what he thought of my performance at the time; my lack of care for the legacy and reputation of the Archbishop of our Province, who was just months from retirement. It's one of my great regrets. The Archbishop really didn't do anything wrong. He trusted, and put faith in me, and although I had vowed to respect his office, I spat on it that day.

But I wasn't done. I knew full well that his retirement was coming, and after Kevin's performance in the Diocesan election, I would no longer be an advisor to the chief in the company. There was a new sheriff in town. The following week, I'd go to Andrew, the newly elected Bishop-in-waiting, and my predecessor at my final parish church. In some ways, I thought I couldn't have hit a bigger jackpot. Andrew's claim-to-fame was that, after an emergency sabbatical in his later years in my parish, he returned, having left his wife. Soon after, he was engaged to a former Sunday school teacher. Many had taken notice that his new fiancée –and her family— had mysteriously disappeared to a neighbouring parish at the beginning of the sabbatical. I did not trust Andrew;

not as far as I could throw the man. But I didn't think for a second,
I'd end up where I am today, knowing how many people worked
to ensure he didn't.

He advised me on how to talk to her father; how to preach
without showing vulnerability to what was happening; and how
to make sure she stayed out of the public eye, eventually telling
me, if I kept my hands off her in public it would all be okay. He
made a joke about how he wished he'd have gotten out front of it
all, the way I had, and then he sent me back to work. I thanked
him, hugged him, and then left to go back to work. This would
be easy. I'm a really good liar. I've had lots of practice at it.

> *"When people in authority want the rest of us to
> behave, it matters—first and foremost—how they
> behave. This is called the 'principle of legitimacy',
> and legitimacy is based on three things. First of all,
> the people who are asked to obey authority have
> to feel like they have a voice—that if they speak
> up, they will be heard. Second, the law has to be
> predictable. There has to be a reasonable expectation
> that the rules tomorrow are going to be roughly the
> same as the rules today. And third, the authority has
> to be fair. It can't treat one group differently from
> another."*

— *Malcolm Gladwell,*
*David and Goliath: Underdogs, Misfits, and the Art
of Battling Giants*

Love

GiffontheWay Blog Post: February 2018.
Written on a bus near the Israeli Syrian border northeast of Caesarea
Philippi.

God's beloved. That is what my name means.

From Saul's anointing of God's chosen King, the
one who would unite the tribes and people.
I met a David today, a young man for whom
I share a name. Nineteen-years-old (looked
even younger) with scruffy auburn hair and an
undeniable look of intrigue. I had just been at
a rest stop, and off the bus, on our way back to
Jerusalem. I had a coffee in my hand and was
taking a deep breath of fresh air before stepping
back aboard. Across the way, the young man
stood next to a camouflaged and armoured jeep.
Dressed in an Israeli uniform, like so many I've
seen on this trip, with a machine gun strapped
across his shoulder in full view. He motioned to
me, and asked me to come over, and I could feel
every eye from my group on the bus look with
panic as I began to step in his direction.
"Where are you from?" he asked, just simply
wanting to engage in some light conversation.

We talked about his military service, his longing to be done, and his plans to settle down with his girl. I told him about my love of the Gospel and how it drove me to want to visit here. He smiled a lot, and was kind and gentle, and nothing like I would have come to expect or fear.

It's hard not to think about a war machine when it rests just inches from you, but I'd certainly reduced the entirety of his humanity to nothing more. I shook his hand and wished him well, and he asked me to pray for him.

David, God's beloved, here in Israel.

#Jesus #Beloved #PrayforPeace

***

If you ask me, "Love" is the most bullshit word in the English language. The wide and varying concept of the English word "love" does not actually exist in and of itself, does it? A word that can describe intimate loving sexual relations between two people in the same breath as favour for pizza toppings or care for one's child. It seems ill-defined to me.

I'm not certain these were his exact words, but Mr. K, my high school English teacher said something very close to this to open a Grade 10 English class: "Love does not exist in the world. Prove me wrong." It was the most provocative and relevant thing I'd ever heard a teacher say, and he had me on the edge of my seat. People responded with answers about loving their parents, or their siblings, or their puppy, and he aggressively defended against each, talking about the persuadability of context, the fickleness of humanity, parental responsibility. He wasn't convinced by what they said. You should have seen people's faces… offended, angry, confused. This was public school, mind you, not the Catholic schools of my past (or future); he had some leeway to work with.

I stuck up my hand and I launched into debate—how in my tradition and in the scriptures of my faith, the word God is synonymous with the word love; that, as John says in his first epistle, God is love. He tried to interrupt me, but I was brave and kept the floor. I referenced the Manitoba flooding of the day, I think, or some current event where disaster had struck not far from home. I told him that, although he might only see disaster on the six o'clock news, I watched further and saw all the first responders reaching the most devastated people and keeping everyone safe. I said, *that's* what God's love looks like in my tradition. Something more like sacrifice.

Mr. K smiled, looked back at me, winked, and looked at the class. He said, open your books to page 25, boys and girls… "Let's see if Mr. Giffen is right about love."

***

I didn't take a lot away from my New Testament Greek class in seminary, but what I did take away was probably the most formative shift in my understanding of what it is to *be Christian*, and how to understand this thing called the Gospel—and it was the word Love. Regardless of whether one speaks of ancient Greek, koine Greek or modern Greek, the sophistication of language with which the Greeks write of love makes us in the English-speaking world look like primitive people.

During my years in active ministry, years when I struggled deeply with the cross-entanglement of intellectual discovery and the defence of my faith, there were not many theologians who I could go to again and again and feel confident I would find helpful answers. Whether it was because topics I wrestled were not written about in other times, or whether they were just not permitted to write about them, I'm not always sure the answer is the same. But in the mid-twentieth century, when the world was tearing itself apart at the seams, an author known for his portrayal of a magic closet to a place called Narnia, was also writing theological treatises by day. *Mere Christianity, The Problem with Pain,* and *The Screwtape Letters* are all books I've come back to countless times. As long as you read C.S. Lewis in context, the same way you would Aristotle or Plato, he humbles himself in his theology, never putting walls around God's grace.

As Lewis so well describes in his book on this topic, *The Four Loves,* the development of my understanding of how we can belong to one another in shared life and community has since been deeply rooted in better understanding of the *language* of love.

The Four Words for Love:

Erōs [Ἔρως]: When I would describe Eros to those who had to endure my preaching, I would joke that it was 'marital' love; which we all know is no guarantee in the long term. So, a better way to describe it might be passionate, sexual love. Not lust, mind you, but an overwhelming yearning to become one with another person, rooted in a sexual desire, but not limited by it. I think we're audaciously lucky when we find someone who we can mutually share a deep and passionate love like this with.

Philia [Φιλία]: Brotherly love, or better described by Lewis as friendship—love between two people who do not share a sexual bond or a familial one, but still live fraternally with one another in love. It seems that this is the rarest kind of love and, as I move into the second half of my life, I am confident and grateful that I am surrounded now by those who offer me this kind of love.

Storgē [Στοργή]: Empathetic love, or affectionate love; often defined as a mother's love. This is the one that always moves me most when I reflect on it, because I had shut it off by the time Rory was born. I shut it off because I thought it was weakness to be emotionally affected so much. When it came back, it came thundering in. But, for those with whom you genuinely share an empathy bond—those whose pain you feel—well, we all need this kind of love.

Agapē [Ἀγάπη]: Sacrificial love. Jesus love. Carry-your-cross love. Give-up-your-life love. Hand-over-your-last-cent love. Selfless love. Unprovoked love. Unconditional love. God love.

***

Less than a year after my ankle fracture, as I limped into my final year as a husband and a priest, I was invited to join clergy from around the world at St George's College in Jerusalem. It was two of the greatest weeks of my life; walking the footsteps of Jesus and entering into the holy sites of three different religious traditions, spanning across thousands of years.

There's no way for me to authentically and redemptively speak about this trip, without first disclosing this: I was high the whole time. I got my hands on a small amount of Oxy before leaving, and because I couldn't take any cannabis with me, my doctor gave me enough sleeping pills to shut a grown man's liver down. It was only the second afternoon when I popped a zopiclone on the bus in the middle of the day. It didn't put me to sleep, but it sure felt euphoric and deep and more intense than it would have otherwise. I know this for sure, because having gone back and looked at my blogs over those few weeks, I grimace, just a little bit. I roamed through the Muslim Quarter of Jerusalem in the middle of the night, trying to find something to eat. I wasn't wild, or causing trouble, or trying to start a fight. I took just the right combination of pain killers and sleeping medication so that, by the end of the trip, there was very little filter on me.

Drugs aside, this trip was a profoundly spiritual experience. I walked the Via Dolorosa holding the arm of an elderly priest, afraid that she might fall. I shed tears with a Palestinian refugee and made lifelong friends with an activist who chooses to stay inside the camp. I saw the humanity of soldiers and discovered truth in the traditions of other faiths.

My drug use doesn't invalidate the experience for me; but it does give it context.

Sitting around a bar, surrounded by newfound friends on one of my last night's there, I told my story aloud for the first time in my life, without fear or filter. I was struggling in lots of different ways. I was unhappy at home and in my job and struggling with undiagnosed traumatic pain. I met a mother figure in Abra, a woman who showed me what *Storgē* looked like again, helped me see it wasn't weak. I met Mabel, who made me smile so much and helped remind me why I first became a priest. I got closer with Aaron, one of my oldest and dearest. It broke my heart to confess to him later that I was using the whole time.

But when I dropped all the details; about my history and childhood and struggles; when I told my authentic story; it was okay. I realized on a rooftop in Jerusalem, overlooking the gates into the historic Old City, that I am my story. That cannot hide from it, not with drugs or alcohol or sex. Repressing what has happened to me and what I've done in my life shatters my*self* into fragmented pieces. It had to end. If anything was ever going to change, I had to accept that my story is painful and real and traumatic in all that it is and was, and I could be loved in spite of it, but more importantly, I could be loved *because of it*.

> "This is what God's kingdom is like: a bunch of outcasts and oddballs gathered at a table, not because they are rich or worthy or good, but because they are hungry, because they said yes. And there's always room for more."
>
> – Rachel Held Evans,
> Searching for Sunday: Loving, Leaving, and Finding the Church

Sin

Some of our earliest references to *sin* are actually not primarily religious. One of the most frequent ancient Hebrew words for sin (חטא, *hata*), used in the Old Testament, was not originally referring to a moral failing or some kind of sentence to death or hell. Instead, it was an archery reference which meant *missing the mark*. If an archer wound back and released an arrow and it missed the target entirely; not just the bull's eye or the outer rims, but if the arrow flew quickly across the sky and didn't get a single piece, it was a sin.

I found it so helpful when I came to realize this. This concept, forced on me in my life, was really just meant to describe *a slip*. A real archer knows that the only way they'll ever miss the target entirely is if something goes sideways – with their equipment, with their body, or with the target itself. A properly trained archer knows a miss that big means something went terribly wrong behind the scenes.

***

Trying to date as a male teenager in my home was impossible. My Dad was never there. My Mum was quite unwell. There were no other boys growing up in the home, and everything *I wanted* seemed to be wrong, all of the time. Apart from that, I was also a disaster with girls.

I would fall in love within weeks of meeting them, desperate for a kind of affection and care that was absent in my life. Then I'd get spooked. I would also fall in love with the most inappropriate or unavailable people and would try to become everything they needed until they loved me. My Mum would make every attempt imaginable to become my girlfriends' best friend; often getting closer to them than I was. She would tell them about how easily they could get pregnant the same way she did (it was way too much information). She would use her pastoral skills to get close to them – in what I have to believe was genuine care. Because –I can't lie about this— as much as I might want to say they all resented her for it, most didn't. Most of them came to love her, quite deeply. Most of them still tell me how grateful they are *to her* for the role she played in their lives. But let's fast-forward and see what happens to the adult mind of a teenage boy being persistently cock-blocked by his mother. It's not a good approach.

Several girls I dated came back to my mother when they had their own mental health breakdowns, some while we were breaking up. She accompanied more than one to treatment at the hospital and maintained friendships with each of them to the horror of the next. People knew. People at my high school, at my church, in my community. They knew. My Mum was too involved in my increasingly non-existent sex life.

The world is just starting to understand the concept of generational trauma – the knowledge that those raised by the traumatized will be traumatized by the trauma of those who raised them. It brings a whole new meaning to the scripture verses (like Numbers 14:18) about the sins of the father being paid onto the sons. It emphasizes how hard those of us who struggle have to work to make sure that our children have all the resources they need to manage the impact of trauma we experienced.

We're starting to scratch the surface on this with large macro understandings of the African slave trade, with its real-life consequences on the world today – and treatment of indigenous people in many parts of the world. I think of my Palestinian friends, for example, who have never been to their ancestral homes, many which have sat empty since the day their parents had to flee. Those who suffer from generational trauma inherit the shame and the consequences of the experiences that shook their forebear to their core, sometimes before a child is even born.

My Mum experienced significant trauma by the time I was born. Sexualized herself at too young an age, pregnant with the first man she chose to sleep with, and an immigrant without support from family in a foreign land where she didn't really want to be. Take away everything that happened in my time with my mother; all her experiences before I was born, the young age she had to start raising me; she was going to instil in me what she knew to instil. Her desire for me not to become the kind of men she feared in her life was an attempt at good. Her desire for me to be a good Catholic boy (maybe even to form me as a celibate priest) … it's messed up, but I understand what she was trying to do. Many of the best men she'd ever known –the ones who didn't harm her and the ones who always cared— they were her priests.

I meet girls today not much older than my Mum was when she came to Canada and I cannot even imagine how they could face what she did. But there is no doubt, her trauma became my trauma became her trauma, in a pretty harmful way.

***

After a screwup at the DMV, and a little maneuvering on my part, I got my hands on an authentic driver's licence that said I was born in 1971 (I'm an '81 child actually). I was just sixteen. I had learned quickly in my little suburban town that unless you were of age, there was very little to do, and no way to get there. My Mum was going through a period of mysterious health breakdowns at the time, and she couldn't get out of bed. My Dad worked a tonne, and frankly, I don't really remember how my sisters were getting fed. There was an assortment of babysitter-type nanny folks over the years, but none ever stayed.

I had a licence to pretty much whatever I wanted, and, at the time, I relished what seemed like a reward. It allowed me to buy and sell alcohol to other minors to make a little cash. This improved my popularity with the *cool kids,* and it allowed me the opportunity to numb the pain. It made me a regular at a local pub on wing night, but it also opened doors to experiences for which I was not healthily prepared.

The first time I heard of *Bunnies,* I was in ninth grade. I overheard a group of senior guys, talking about one of their nineteenth birthdays... how wasted everyone was and how they had a "VIP Room" ... how the birthday boy had quite the time.

Remember: I grew up with a very particular lens on sex, and this introduction to public school life was a shock to my system. Frankly, I thought it was amazing, like many fourteen-year-old boys would. Strip clubs were not something I even knew existed at the time. I was a sheltered kid in this respect. I wasn't allowed to watch GI Joe or 90210 or anything with violence or sex. Hearing older boys talk about what they did with their weekend blew my mind and made me want to know more. I had no idea what I was looking for, but I looked it up in the yellow pages and found it right there. Strip Club, right in the middle of the industrial complex not more than a ten-minute bike ride from my house. I must have ridden my bike there once a week to sit across the street, just to gaze and wonder what was happening inside. Every once in a while, someone would come out for a smoke, and I'd get a glimpse of this very different life.

But when my fake ID had sat in my wallet for not more than a week, I decided it was time for me to go in. I'd had a couple of sexual experiences at this point. But for the most part, I had very little idea what I was doing. Also, I really didn't care if I got caught. I was angry and arrogant and messed up inside, and more than willing to get someone's attention. So, one day, I came home from lunch, put on the leather jacket I'd been given for Christmas and grabbed the keys to my Mum's car. No one was going to notice, because shit was so sideways at this point anyway, that nothing seemed out of place.

I pulled up into the parking lot and got out with a deep breath. The bouncer looked at my ID, smiled, said, "Have fun son," and ushered me in. I couldn't believe it worked, to be honest. I thought it was the biggest risk I could take. Not because getting caught would have gotten me in so-much-shit, but because I would have lost my ID. I ordered whatever beer was first suggested and grabbed a seat. It was dark; and my eyes took a few minutes to adjust. There was porn on the TV – not soft porn, actual hardcore porn, the kind I'd only ever seen on the fuzzy channels at 2 a.m. Everything about this place was the freaking bizarro world, and that's when she sat down next to me. She said I was cute. She asked me for "a dance" and said it was twenty dollars a song. I couldn't believe it. I thought I was just going to just see a show. Twenty dollars a song! That's it?!

I walked up the steps and into the VIP area and she closed the door to a small room. She danced for me and then on top of me, and then slowly without her clothes. She unbuckled my pants and sat on top of me and put me inside of her. Six seconds maybe? Before I came. No condom. No discussion. Just fucked. She got off me and started to re-dress and told me it would be two hundred dollars. I didn't know what to do. She said twenty dollars a song, didn't she? I started to try and explain. I told her I didn't have that kind of cash. She looked angry and so I told her she could have my new leather jacket and it was worth about the same.

She picked it up, and left the room, and I never saw her again

***

I have struggled to maintain an ongoing sexual relationship throughout every stage of my life. With my beautiful ex-wife when she was in her early twenties and in no relationship that lasted more than six weeks since. I went through periods where the only sex I had was with high-end escorts who I paid for with my father's bank account or making friends with dancers from the local strip club. I was terminated from my job, and deprived of ministry as a priest, because I entered into a secret sexual relationship with someone who worked for me.

Let's be clear here, I am not blaming Heather or my Mum or some exotic dancer from when I was just a teen. It doesn't work that way. Maybe I wish it did. I have to take responsibility for anything I've done wrong, and any consequence it's had on me or others. As do they. But my inability to find sexual intimacy unless I believe it to be wrong... well, good luck building a nice little Christian family. I've had some incredible sex and some exciting encounters, but they are almost always followed by deep shame and extended periods of guilt and self-loathing, pain and suicidal thoughts from my inability to fulfill my marriage vows. Wanting to love my wife from a place of duty –in the ways she deserved to be loved— but never being able to.

The sexual ethics of the Church however, across denominations, need to change dramatically. We can no longer credibly say we don't know about the harm closeting sexuality has done. Teaching plain readings of monogamy or fidelity is a fine approach, but no child should ever grow up being afraid of their body, or the pleasure that's discovered there, or the desires they have to share their sexuality (never mind that choices they make will send them to hell).

I'm not sure I can say I was raped as a sixteen-year-old boy, because on some level I knew what I was doing. But it changed me. I know that – likely forever and it's a memory that won't fade.

But the memory no longer haunts me the way it once it did with the shame and the guilt and the self-loathing. At this stage in my life, having become quite close friends with men and women currently working in the sex industry, I have learned to remember my memories in ways that now look for the story beyond my own. I even started to pray for her for a time. We all find ourselves crashing into one another with all our histories of baggage and pain. I hope she found peace and happiness on her journey, this woman without a name.

> *"You may be surprised who you find in heaven. God has a soft spot for sinners, his standards are actually quite low."*
>
> *— Archbishop Desmond Tutu,*
> *2009 Festival of Homiletics, Atlanta, Georgia*

Giffen vs. the World

When I was a teenager, I wrote a lot of poetry. Mostly in an attempt to try and get girls to sleep with me, but also because it was a way for me to articulate my experience of the world. It was a form of journaling most of the time, and certainly my attempt to make sense of the reality I faced. I penned this piece just a few weeks after my first case of alcohol poisoning at Rory's Uncle Donny's sixteenth birthday party. I made a fool of myself in front of his girlfriend's older sister and ended up covered in vomit in their bathtub.

The poem would later be published in my college years by a magazine; my father refused to buy a copy or even look at it.

> Liquid courage,
> From the empty bottle,
> Smashed to the asphalt.
>
> Said is what we mean to say,
> But not what we felt yesterday,
> Or what we will remember tomorrow.
> Clumps of sand lay in the throat,
> Yet words proclaim their glory.
> But not glory.
> For glory is of victory,
> Not of insecurity.

I am insecure,
Broken among the glass,
Scattered to the asphalt.

I do not drink of the cup of Judas,
Nor the cup of Christ.

Still I search myself in bottle where I do not rest,
And satisfy myself with false satisfaction,
Slurping on my liquid courage.

Yeah, nothing to see here.

***

After my first case of alcohol poisoning, I endured a 90-day grounding. No telephone, friends, or leaving my house without a parent. I was fifteen, so my choice was obvious: I would skip as many classes as I could, to go get high or have beers with my friends, because when else was I supposed to do it? How my friends got away with skipping class, I'm not sure. But I had the automatic phone call sequence from the office deactivated with a forged note to the administrator to change our home phone number. Effie would never skip class, so it wasn't like they were getting any other calls.

After the grounding was over, right through the end of high school, I really did become a bit of a menace. There's no getting around it at this point. It got so bad, that when my friends organized the senior guys' trip to Acapulco, Donny had to tell me it would be a good idea if I sat this one out. No one wanted to be responsible for my safety.

One Friday night, after way too many shots of Johnny Walker Red Label (the cheapest Scotch I could get my hands on, and otherwise known to my friends as Giff's *fight juice*), there was a group of us walking to the historic Duchess of Markham pub. As we walked down Main Street, a guy I'd been lippy to the week prior caught a passing glimpse of me.

"Hey! You red sack of shit. Get over here!"

There had been an altercation the week before, and Snowball's extra six-inches of height and pro-lacrosse-playing build would certainly make me think twice, but probably not a third time. The weekend before, Snowball had brushed past me in the park on Friday night, just the wrong way, to which I responded, "*Your Mom.*" That's all I really needed to say to these guys. My very presence pissed some of them off, whether they admitted it or not. I didn't play a single sport after I 'sprained my ankle' in Grade 11 rugby, but all my best friends were still the jocks. It never sat well with my football-loving, hockey-player-raising hometown. As though there was something strange about someone because they learned the words of poets got a girl's attention, no different than skates.

Also, I have no pain tolerance. None. The first football practice with pads in Grade 9 almost killed me. I was happy to leave contact sports behind, unless of course Red Label was in avail.

Snowball went after me, and he almost landed a punch. He turned back to come at me again and there was Sheldon right up in his face. As big as Snowball was, Sheldon appeared bigger. Snowball almost bounced off him as he tried to come at me. Sheldon stared him down, and all his friends right with him. He didn't say a word for almost twenty seconds; then he looked at them, speaking with his football captain's voice and shaking his head: "You want a piece of Giffen? You go through me."

I have never fully understood why Sheldon chose to be my big brother. In many ways, as I've told him, he raised me (to be fair to him, the clay was fairly well molded by the time it was his turn). He taught me maturity (as best he could), how not to be an ass, and he's forgiven me more times than I'd care to count. But never has he failed to stand up for me, regardless of whether I'm wrong, right, or out in left field.

I look back now, and I realize that I wasn't okay when I was a teenager. I was constantly medicating with drugs and alcohol and sex and getting my face kicked in. I could barely breathe anywhere in my home; it's why I had to move out of my house in my senior year.

But, when I needed it most, I learned how to be a little brother, and how to have someone stick up for me.

***

"It is better to be feared than loved."
— *Niccolò Machiavelli*

"If troops lay siege to a walled city, their strength will be exhausted."
— *Sun Tzu*

"The ends justify the means."
— *Niccolò Machiavelli*

"Regard your soldiers as your children, and they will follow you into the deepest valleys. Look on them as your own beloved sons, and they will stand by you even unto death!"
— *Sun Tzu*

By the time I finished my first year of university, I had read *The Prince*, by Machiavelli, and *The Art of War*, by Sun Tzu, at least ten times each. I had never actually identified with Jesus, from the gospel stories. Frankly, he was way too righteous for someone like me. I was more like a tax collector playing his role behind the scenes in the gospel stories, or maybe at times like a revolutionary wanting to burn the Empire down. Jesus did speak to me in lots of ways. I just never felt *like* him, as I saw displayed in the lives of so many of the beloved Christians, I had the privilege to serve as priest.

Who did I feel like? You guessed it! Those *other* guys. The ones up top of the page. The ones who made me feel strong for being smart. The ones who helped me see that I could continuously have the upper hand. The ones who could help me define victory over defeat. The ones that—*regardless of what anyone wants to think or say now*—made me incredibly successful in the current culture of ministry.

For most of my adult life, I lived my life by going to war every single day, by creating a world of allies and adversaries for whom engagement with, and the process of how, would already be laid out in careful plays. I learned to play four to six moves ahead of everyone else in my life: at my church, at home, and with my extended family. I was constantly using people to gain advantage. Making moves behind the scenes. I had made a decision, long ago, never to allow myself to feel emotions again (good luck!), while seeking to win the daily war I faced. It was a plan, a fine one. I wasn't going to feel anymore. I was going to achieve more. We were going to feed more people. My church would be bigger. More money would start to flow in. The ends justified the means, almost regardless of what I did.

I knew leadership. I learned it from my mother and my father and then from Rory's uncles, Donny, Rob and Sheldon. Eventually, I'd take my cues from this guy Jesus, but in between, I learned it from great warriors, prophets and philosophers, like Wallace of Scotland 700 years ago or Dr. King in Selma before he proclaimed his dream.

Let me be clear: I believe that if the world could live the message of the Gospel—the banquet table where the poor are honoured, and kings take off their crowns—it would be ideal. I believe the scriptures of my people, and, in some rare instances, I see them alive and at work in the Church today. But I learned quickly that the kind of docile leadership found in the Gospel wasn't a skill that made a *success*.

To be clearer: It *might* make for a successful church, but rarely a successful priest.

It was made clear to me, by almost every superior, at almost every stage of priestly formation and development: Leadership, from a new perspective, was a skill lacking across the board. So, I leaned into it, and through it, and around it, and on top of it, and I had every opportunity and advantage handed to me, because of the skills of the prophets *Mach & Tzu*—and no one argued with the results until my collar was taken from me.

Looking back, I justified all of it, by the fact that I was going to war for *the betterment of humanity*, and to build up the *Kingdom of God*. I hear myself say it now, and I shake my head. I did do really good work. I led churches that fed thousands of marginalized people every year. I empowered sexual minorities to come to the table and share in the Eucharist. I fought for the rights of those who couldn't fight for themselves. But I used every tactic and every skill I would have learned at a strategic leadership conference to do it; my skills were not really flowing from the heart of Gospel. I had completely convinced myself that my messed-up brain could be redeemed somehow, if I just made the world a less messed-up place.

This is why regardless of all my sins—and there are many—I still go to confession, even today. I have always been more aware than I would have liked to be of my own deficits, of all the places I don't really measure up. But it was always in confession that I experienced the generous heart of God. Knowing that someone else knew how bad it all really was—that, even in all my own failures, I could still be redeemed.

Grace & Mercy

"Grace is when you get what you don't deserve,
And mercy is when you don't get what you do
deserve."

— Bishop William G. Cliff

I met Father Bill Cliff when I was an undergraduate student at King's University College, one of the Catholic affiliate colleges at Western University in London, Ontario. Bill was the Anglican Chaplain across campus when I was starting off there writing papers entitled, *In Defense of Heresy*. I hadn't won any points –with any of the Priests or the Nuns– when in front of the student body, I said, "Jesus could probably make himself sixty percent available in a rice cracker, if wheat bread wasn't available for the Eucharist". I was only there because my first two kicks at the undergraduate can had failed miserably with a car crash, and then a lot of weed. King's had a really low threshold for admittance, and I had been able to secure some solid reference letters, as I've always had the ability to make my way through a door. But now that I was here, studying Roman Catholic theology, I wasn't going to toe the line.

Bill made a different kind of space for a young, struggling student like myself. He didn't have a code of conduct I needed to live by (right away) or a set of beliefs I had to profess on day one. He just made space and recognized how much hurt there was out there. He sought to welcome any prodigals home. I recognized quickly that I was more at home in his Chapel than I'd ever been in any church. The words of the Gospel made sense to me here, and I recognized the stories of Jesus far more than I had ever connected with the morality driven theological treatises of my upbringing. Bill believed in grace, more than anything else, and mercy not far behind. He defined them as when you get what you don't deserve, and when you don't get what you do deserve. This guy made sense.

I had been raised in a home where *deserve* and *earn* were the cornerstones of the foundation. My Dad did not believe in hand-outs or receiving charity. You had to work for what you would get. I now better understand his Scottish Presbyterian work ethic. He came by it honestly, and the man really did pull himself up by his bootstraps. My grandmother was the local school custodian and he started working for money at eight. Dad always had the ability to work hard, save and earn, and although he'd be oblivious to the fact, it was almost impossible for me to be motivated in his 'prosperous' home, never mind by the same method that lit a fire under him in poverty. In our house, I needed to earn everything I got, and if I achieved something, that is how I would know it was earned.

When I heard the old definitions of the basic tenets of my faith in terms of grace and mercy, it all made sense. None of us could actually pull ourselves up by our bootstraps; that's why my Dad has always struggled in lots of ways unseen, quite mightily. Deep down he knows he was given opportunities he didn't earn, financial compensation he didn't deserve. His work ethic and worldview were devoid of community, family, or God. Dad wanted to be our only community, family, or God. We were taught not to rely on grace or mercy, because instead, we should rely on hard work, determination, and most of all, him.

There is a parable in chapter 20 of the Gospel of Matthew, when Jesus describes workers in a vineyard who got paid the same for working all day long as those who showed up in the last hour of the day. I remember the first time I read it to my Dad. He said it must have been a bad translation, and it couldn't possibly mean what I said. I've always thought he was more inclined to put his faith in something more like a version of 'karma'. If you're a hard worker and you put the hours in, you should get well paid. If you are a degenerate homeless person, you should eat your mess.

I had plenty of opportunities to rebut this in ministry, and I would tip-toe around it with my Dad. But Christians shouldn't believe in a distorted view of karma: What goes around does not come around, in our faith. We believe the heart of the Gospel says something very different; that Jesus has far lower standards than my father or the Church. You can find forgiveness and start anew from *anywhere*, after *anything*. Our God is a foolish God, whose love has never known bounds.

I'll join that church again when it opens. Keep me posted, I might try and bring some family.

***

There were many nights in high school when I came home as a drunken emotional wreck at two in the morning. There was the night I came home with cuts all over my face from a faceplant into the sidewalk outside of Billy Cees. The night I came home almost unable to walk, because I'd had the shit kicked out of me. There was the night I came home and shattered the basement window trying to break in, and there was the night I came home utterly destroyed because the girl I was sleeping with had ended it with me.

I was seventeen years old and she was nineteen. She was beautiful and emotional and damaged just like I was. She stayed up all night on the phone with me –almost every night of the week–and kept me a secret from her older boyfriend. I never realized how wrong this situation was, because she said she was in love with us both. I look back now and can fully recognize how infatuated I was; I would have broken the law for her. She became my best friend, and then my lover, and then we practically set in as each other's therapists. But when she had arrived at my family home a week earlier, in tears, my Mum said she needed help. She was cutting, and self-harming and she opened up about everything at our kitchen table. My Mum asked her if she wanted to go to the hospital and she said yes.

She broke it off with me when she got out. She needed to focus on her health and her *actual* boyfriend. I was more broken-hearted than I have ever been since, and I genuinely believed the world was coming to an end. My Dad tried to get me to suck it up and stop crying, telling me I was way better off without this headcase, while my Mum screamed from the other room that it was my fault for having sex with someone else's girlfriend. I *deserved* the pain I felt.

I lived in shame, guilt, pain —so much the time— and I believed that I deeply deserved it too.

I understood that I was somehow defective or broken or just simply bad, and that's why so much shit happened to me. It was the best explanation for why they thought I was so deviant and why I was always getting yelled at. It's why I'd steal from their liquor cabinet or my Dad's wallet and would always seem to attract a fist to punch in my face. I stopped caring about consequences, and started self-medicating at a very young age, because I didn't think anything I could do, or not do, would actually change my fate. When you're bad, you're just bad. Not like a villain so much as a defective toy that wasn't properly made.

Shame… guilt… pain. They formed me in deeper ways than faith or love at times. I believed, *religiously*, that I deserved what I got when I got it, regardless of whether I understood why or how. And, I didn't earn much, just ask my Pop. That's why I played into my role, and I stole and lied without conscience or integrity. Because I was what I was, and I wasn't going to change. I was formed in this mindset of shame-based theology, and it stayed with me long after my teenage years. It has always played at least a subconscious part in my decision-making. Even today, I choose to act against instinct much of the time, because I'm aware that what I was formed in does not necessitate my continued belief or adherence.

Not long after we got married and I was ordained a priest, my workaholism and inattentiveness to my marriage led my young bride to look elsewhere to fill my constantly empty seat. It's one of the few times I lost emotional control of myself in my late twenties —and came very close to a complete breakdown. When the new family I had chosen *for the rest of my life* couldn't stay faithful to me. I shouldn't have been all that surprised, and I'm certainly not now knowing the effects of generational trauma, but I was ill equipped to be a husband to Heather in the ways she had a right to expect me to be.

I made a conscious decision to compartmentalize Heather's *indiscretion* and repress any feelings of betrayal or resentment. Because I knew I deserved what happened to me. It was my fault, obviously. It had always been. I was unable to be who she needed me to be, and so why shouldn't she go elsewhere to find it? I was lucky she wasn't choosing to leave. Heeding the mantra of my childhood, *"Don't tell anyone,"* I suppressed all of it and *dug in and kept going* as my Dad would have advised. I never told a soul beyond my confessor. Not my best friends, or my colleagues, or my family. I knew if I did, my marriage would likely end; because shit would go sideways, just like it always did.

It took years before I'd even say I forgave her; because I'd choose to stop feeling after that. I would not be weak. I would not lose everything I had *earned* because my defectiveness had made me *deserve* worse. My self-loathing was at a climax, and I knew that we'd never be the same. But I wasn't going to get divorced before thirty (good luck achieving anything as a priest). Instead I would be the man my Dad raised me to be. I would dig in.

***

I have stolen from, manipulated and lied to my father since I was a child. In the early years, it was because I didn't think it made a difference; in my teens it was because I thought he deserved it; and as an adult it was masked in necessity. He wanted me to be married to someone like Heather, to live a quiet, peaceable life, and not disturb the new life he had made.

Eventually, he actually loved me in Holy Orders. Not at first mind you, as he said that I was squandering every opportunity he had worked to create for me. But when he saw the discipline and order religious life called for, and when my public chaos diminished for enough consecutive years —when I learned to mask all that afflicted me— it was actually the result he'd always been hoping to see. I remember the summer after I discovered Heather was having an affair; the entire family was at his cottage; present were more of his wife's relatives than ours. Someone asked my Dad what he thought of the vows – of marriage and priesthood— that I'd made at such a young age, and his response was that if he could have gotten me married and in religious orders when I was sixteen, it would have saved him a lot of money, stress, and headache.

"What a dink!" I thought to myself, as if that's how he answers the question.

My father paid for every penny of my education. He paid for half my wedding and gave me thousands of dollars every year. But ironically, I was never out of debt once in my married life, and I was rarely happily married. His life was better because I was who I was now, so he made sure I would stick to my promises and not relinquish anything. It didn't matter how hard I told him life got; shingles, fractures, insomnia, pancreatitis, my body was constantly yelling at me. Dad only ever had one piece of advice: Dig in! He didn't know any different, and he thought by paying for golf memberships, vacations, and toys, I would eventually just fit in. But I have always resented him. Resented the control, the money, the arrogance, and my need to keep my mouth shut, because of how badly I came to rely on all he would provide.

But here's the problem I face, and it's a big one. I believe in *grace* and *mercy* – as cornerstones maybe even more important than *love*. I have been a complete failure at showing my father what I have always wanted him to show me.

Godparents

On the day of my baptism in 1981, before I was even a month old, my godparents were named. My mother's 14-year-old brother, my godfather Brian, and my mother's best friend from childhood, my godmother Karen. Three Catholic teenagers (and my Protestant father) making baptismal commitments on behalf of a three-week-old child none of them could have fathomed a year earlier.

Like my experience of much of my Scottish family, I never got to know my godparents very well. I love them. I was grateful to visit with them when we could. I was genuinely touched by the cross-Atlantic gifts sent for my birthdays and Christmases, but truthfully, they didn't really play an active role in my life. This is true of most of my Scottish family. In the 80's, there was no FaceTime or email or other digital forms of communication. Telephone calls were very expensive and handwritten letters don't tend to connect deeply with children under ten. However, I didn't really know any different, outside of the pre-cognitive experiences of infancy and early childhood. I never knew adults, other than my parents, who were meant to be trusted and safe to share struggles and stumbles with.

That is what I found in the Church: a place to call home. People who had rituals and traditions. Extended family, who were often strange and beloved in such eccentric ways. Which is why my Mum – and me – always seemed to fit in. I have now lived at 33 different addresses in my 39 years on this earth. In poor back corners in my earliest years, and in orchard dream houses of marble and exotic stone in my teens. I wanted *home* to be with

Heather, but I just didn't know how. I now know home is with Rory —more than anyone else— but I also believed for a significant period of my adult life, that I belonged to the Church more than I even belonged to him.

This description is not an uncommon experience for many Canadian immigrants, especially those who don't come from the UK; leaving a life behind to start a new one in a new world. This is why Canadian immigration continues to keep churches full too, and why the Anglican church seems to be dying. Macedonian Orthodox communities, Filipino Catholic communities. Look at the eras and locations of immigration across Canada, and where the denominational churches and mosques that spring up. When you have no roots, the Church does adopt you and gives you deeper roots than you ever imagined before. When I put a stole on behind an altar and elevated a loaf of bread, I believed I was 2000 years old; no longer just myself, but something much more.

For a kid who grew up with bleeding gums, extended hospital check-ins, and hives all over his body half the time, it's really no wonder I didn't learn the basics of family life. Rory's uncle Rob still recounts days when my teeth would bleed at sleepovers, and all the other kids would point it out. Dozens of moldy pop cans under my bed. The lack of any real discipline or structure for seasons, instead of days or weeks. Sitting in the boardroom of my Dad's office for eight consecutive hours on a Saturday, and then doing it all over again the next day (to my parents credit, this was orchestrated so we could have a meal with him on the weekend and give my Mum a bit of peace). You'd think it would be hard to have someone else know and tell you these stories about your life, as I give Rob licence to in ways I don't give to many people. But when family disappears, regardless of the reason, someone to help attest to the narrative of your life —the good, the bad, *and* the ugly— matters a great deal.

That is why, when it came to picking godparents, during the height of my time in religious life, I chose the two people Heather and I knew to be people of great character and resilient strength, people with a likeness to a first-century rabbi I used to spend a lot of time talking about. We didn't seek out candidates from her family or mine, or old friends from decades ago. I desperately wanted to know that, no matter what happened in any of his familial relationships, Rory's godparents would be the ones who would always respond to him from the fountain of God's grace, as they have arduously responded for me. I chose solid, intelligent, gospel-proclaiming church people—people who when the Church tarred and feathered me, at great cost to themselves, stood next to me.

But most of Rory's recollective life has been outside of the Church. Since leaving ministry just before he turned five, most of his memories will be absent of the life I thought I was choosing for him as a PK ("Priest's Kid"). I wanted him to know belonging, in a way I hadn't really known it as a kid; roots that ran deep into the soil of history and story that would inspire him to lead a life of significance and greatness. It wasn't relationships I wanted for him, because so many of mine either weren't real or didn't exist anymore. Instead, I could aim for legacy.

I look back now, not really all that long afterwards, and I think it's such a crock of shit. I realize how much my father's worldview impacted mine, especially when I could see myself emulating him as a Dad. I was raised by a man who grew up in abject poverty, and by his bootstraps made millions through genuine hard work and an unshakable belief that he was always the smartest man in the room. I learned first-hand what the ascendancy from an eight-year-old milk and newspaper delivery boy looks like when he grows up helping to keep the rent paid and the lights on – to then battle for capital gains as a board room strategist who made a career on bullying a room. You don't get to be in my father's life, unless you bend the knee. It took a long time for me to accept that, but the only way I'll ever stand in his presence again is if he'll see us on the same level and he can look at the real me.

There's a scene in the movie *The Darkest Hour*, when Winston Churchill becomes Prime Minister during the opening salvo of World War II. His devoted and supportive wife makes a toast to the old man, in front of their many children who have all known his absence in their lives. She admits that when she married him, she knew that public life would always demand Winston's attention before that of the family, and on this day, they would toast him and *their sacrifice*, for the good of the nation. I mention this scene, because I imagine it is what my father would have loved to have experienced, and likely believes he deserves. The great pioneer, who took off from Scotland with his teenage wife and child to make a name for himself in the new world – never to return to Scotland, poverty, or helplessness ever again. The worshipped patriarch of the family.

But I chose to be, largely because I wanted, a different kind of Dad.

When my marriage and career –my life as a priest and role in the community– were stripped from me, I could have used some godparents. I needed a home. People who would care for me and keep me safe, both from myself and from the world. I needed to collapse for a while, into the arms of a mother or father, or aunt, uncle, or grandparents. Someone who was less concerned about all that I'd done wrong, and more concerned with getting me off the ground. Someone whose shared history with me didn't set off emotional and psychological grenades of old trauma in recurring wounds.

As I hit my first birthday on the other side of my collapse, I thanked God for what I'd found in my 38th catastrophic trip around the sun... what I learned about family and community and the very centre of love; grateful to start again.

GiffontheWay Blog Post: May 2019.
Written in a coffee shop on Bloor Street in the heart of Toronto.

I've had quite the opportunity to take stock this last year, and as I leap into my thirty-ninth journey around the sun, there are some things I think I'm finally starting to understand.

Relationships are what matter most. It doesn't seem to matter how much one succeeds or achieves or earns, it is who you love and how much you love that will resound far louder in the echoes of our common life.

People are at the core of relationships. This may sound obvious, but my iPhone updated me on my screen-time last week and although I connect with countless people through my devices, I do fear some days that I have a deeper relationship with the device than I do the person on the other end.

We all need family. Family isn't the same for everyone, but at a very basic level, we all need people who know our story, love us both for and in spite of it, and call us out on our bullshit when we wade too far into uncharted waters or blustery storms.

God is more faithful in the darkness than I ever needed him to be in the light. I woke up on my birthday to the sound of a little boy filled with joy at the crack of dawn, desperately wanting me to hear the words "Happy Birthday" as my first experience of this new year. Rory's Mom baked a cake, raised a glass, and brought our boy to experience his father's 38th with some of his oldest friends. And my childhood brothers – the ones I knew when I still wet the bed (shut up Rob – I was not eight!) – they gathered in my home, celebrated my life, and reminded me where I come from.

God is faithful. Even when I don't see the light.

Last but not least: Love matters.

When everything else gets stripped away. When all that's left is the years that have passed and an unknown journey that lies ahead: Love matters. Not so much romantic love or familial love or brotherly love, but a love that Jesus liked to talk about.

Love that's offered without considering cost or measure and received without debt.

God's love on my birthday. Thankful and blessed.

***

I woke up, startled. The smell of the merlot across the countertop –drenched into the grout of the kitchen floor— was overwhelming. My eyes could barely open and the sound of my iPhone erupting felt like an attack upon my cranium. I threw the phone across the room and buried my head underneath a mountain of covers. It was Monday morning. The day after I had been publicly accused of sexual exploitation by a member of my church staff. The day after I was scarlet-lettered and publicly ridiculed by the senior most Bishop in my province, in front of hundreds of people, across four services, in my large, downtown, urban parish.

The first bottle of wine got uncorked early that morning, and no glass was necessary. By Noon, I'd melt down on social media. By three, I'd tell all my loved ones to *go fuck themselves*. By nine, I had done everything I could do to wipe my significant digital presence from across the web. By midnight, I wouldn't be alone (if you count a stranger in my bed). But, by the time the phone awoke, early the next morning, I was half-naked, I smelled atrocious, and I was excruciatingly alone. Frankly, I wasn't sure if I really wanted to move ever again. My phone rang twice more. I actually yelled, "Fuck off!" at the top of my lungs. I didn't care who it was, really didn't. I couldn't give a single shit what anyone needed. I was done. On so many different levels. Broken, in ways I had seen too often, in too many who had come to me for counsel during my decade as a parish priest.

There was a loud knock at my door. I jumped out of bed. "What have I done?!" I thought to myself, trying desperately to re-trace fuzzy memories of the day before; instinctively trying to find a place to hide. There it was again, louder this time. "Open the door!" I heard from the other side. I had heard this voice, throughout some of the most important moments of my life, but in that moment, all I could hear was the terror that emanated from a soul that had been stripped of much of its perceived identity.

I opened the door just a crack, and standing there, gazing at my dishevelled face, were my three closest friends from childhood – the same men I'd come to refer to as Uncles to my son. They didn't say a word. I turned around and walked back into my tiny bachelor apartment dominated by the massive king-sized bed, I couldn't really afford. I sat down, they stood at the foot, I dropped my head in shame, and I started to try and explain.

I was in love with her. I was so miserable at home. My broken ankle and the addiction to painkillers. She was a lot younger than me. She said she wanted to be with me! I didn't know it would unravel like this. "I didn't…" I continued down a road trying to explain how I could have let this all happen; how I could have fallen so far. But Sheldon didn't let me finish. He wouldn't let me utter another word. He put up his hand, almost right in my face, and said, "David. We don't care if you're guilty. We love you either way."

Off Ramps

The initial year after my parents' separation—as they split assets and my Dad opened his chequebook—it had far less consequence on me than it did on my sisters. I had moved out of my family home the summer before my last year of high school, and I tried to limit the extent of my involvement in family life to the path of least resistance that would maintain my hold on the Jeep (which I'd soon destroy) and keep my rent paid. My Dad was more than willing to keep me funded, as long as I worked to keep family peace.

It shouldn't have been, but it was a surprise to me when I came home the following summer and saw how messed up the whole dynamic had become. My sisters really didn't get any proper cues from me in the years prior. It will likely be the biggest failure of my entire life—my choice, as a young adult, to abdicate my role to help them understand what was happening to our family. There were a lot of tears and a lot of fights and a lot of threats about who would do what to whom if someone didn't move here, or pay for that, or threaten anyone else's right to anyone or anything. I'm serious. Shit can go off the rails, especially when you thought you knew what that meant, and you really didn't.

My Mum arrived at her former family home, which was now my Dad's primary residence. My parents started to argue, and my Mum lost her temper, while my Dad stayed calm enough to push every one of her buttons. She was supposed to be picking up my youngest sister, and I had seen this reel too many times before. I felt my neck become hot and my face started to sweat, and I yelled, "You're not taking her!" How on earth this was *my role* in this situation is ridiculous to even consider, so I pray I can avoid history ever repeating itself. I got between my parents and forbade my Mum from taking my sister with her, and her face was overcome with fear. She was one hundred percent triggered in her own traumatic stress injuries in this moment, as two grown men were telling her she was not allowed to take her child. .

As a father with a beloved son today, and as a man who struggles with mental health, my heart breaks for her in this situation. She screamed at me and tried to push me out of the way, and my Dad yelled, "Don't hit her back." She started hitting him, and when I tried to break it up, she hit me with a nearby tennis racquet. I took her keys, went into the backyard and I threw them in the pool. She screamed, I ran, and then she jumped in the water after them. The neighbours could see from their backyard deck. My Dad looked like he was losing his mind, and my mother was in the pool with her clothes on.

I called 911. I called for an ambulance. I called because we— as a family—were having a mental health crisis. My sisters ran and hid. We didn't see them again for hours. My Mum was taken in the back of a cop car in front of the gathered neighbourhood— because they sent squad cars well before an ambulance. There wasn't a social worker anywhere to be seen. In the end, no charges were filed, and a peace bond was made, but it is no wonder I lived most of my life with the firm and unshakable belief that conflict, and emotional outbursts, will bring the world to a crashing halt, and the walls will eventually close in.

***

During a group therapy session in Nashville, after sharing a number of these stories with friends made in treatment there, it became an ongoing joke that my life could be synopsized by showing the same recurring film reel on repeat.

It went something like this:

> *David gets on the highway. David notices signs saying the highway is coming to an end. David notices that everyone else is getting off the highway. David speeds up. David passes the first off-ramp. David notices a service station by the side of the road. David ignores it. David notices the engine is on fire. David steps on the gas. David passes by the final off-ramp on the highway and —at full speed— crashes the car directly into a wall. But David's not done. David then invites everyone he knows to come and see the mess. Good talk or bad talk, as long as they're talking, it seems.*

I really needed to re-evaluate.

Your life doesn't need to devolve into the ninth circle of hell. There is almost always an off-ramp way before that. Yet, for most of my life, I have rarely chosen them.

***

Within days of meeting with the Bishops to disclose varying degrees of truth about my misconduct, I was on the floor of my bedroom in my family home, a bottle deep for the first time in nine and a half years. I know addicts who don't believe me when I say this, but with all the addictive tendencies and self-medicating strategies I continued to struggle with during my ten years of ordained ministry, I quit drinking the year I was ordained and I didn't sip another drop of non-transubstantiated ferment until that summer I fell apart. My life and relationships were breaking down under the pressure and, one-by-one, every aspect of my life began to implode. I could see the grip I once had on everything, holding on so tight *because I knew* that if I gave just an inch, I would lose it all. Most therapists would say I was catastrophizing, but only I knew the faulty foundation my life had been built on. Only I knew how little it would take to collapse.

Heather found me and kicked me out before Rory got home, and I ended up a fifth of vodka deeper, downtown at the Royal York Hotel. At midnight, I couldn't handle it anymore. I knew I was done. I knew it was going to get a whole lot worse. I knew the coming years were going to be treacherously hard. I've never been much of a prophet, and I couldn't have told you all the details ahead of time, but I knew this wasn't going to end well. I reached out to Rory's godparents in the middle of the night from a street corner downtown, and within an hour Jeff had me in his car. They fed me, hydrated me, and made no conditions for what I had to do next. They loved me and genuinely wanted me to stay with them and let them take care of me, but they were an off-ramp way too early. I didn't know how to accept their help, because I don't know what it's like to go home to be safe. I'm just starting to learn the baby steps of it now. Allowing someone else to clothe and feed me, and make sure I'm not destroying myself in the middle of an acute crisis … allowing someone else to take responsibility for me while I heal. It was on offer from them. I could have chosen it, and if I had, I would probably still be a priest. But I would still be lying to myself—and to my son—about the very core of my identity.

Jeff and Becky are the guardian angels of my life, and Rory's chosen godparents. They have always allowed me to be exactly who I am, and they know I finish my day laying down my shortfalls before God. I left the next day, knowing I would never be able to get through this on my own, but that didn't seem to matter anymore. Between the many medicators I was using at this point, the relief from the pain was something I might have defended even to death. It was time I stepped away from being a priest. I phoned Bishop Kevin and told him where I was and what had happened and how I was drinking again. The next day I went on medical leave.

This was the first off ramp I'd taken in a very long time, but my nature is what it has always been, and I couldn't stay out of the car.

I've battled with church authorities since the month I left active ministry. I was accused and investigated and found guilty of sexual misconduct. I was using and medicating at a pace I hadn't since my teens. I gave no consideration to consequences or reputation. I fought privately and publicly and digitally and legally. The top search for my name on Google—until we fought to have it taken down—was a newsletter article by the interim priest-in-charge of my parish, telling the world I'd been accused of sexual exploitation with no context, follow-up or explanation. You can imagine what over a year of this exposure did for my career opportunities.

I was shown the door and handed a steaming pile of crap to take with me. I was a threat to episcopal authority. I was flagrant about it the whole time. Now, looking back, I wish I hadn't been, and I know I've always been a lippy little weasel in a fight. But it's the reason I won't ever veer right and get out of this car on this particular road. I've been told numerous times that if I would just shut my mouth and go away for a couple of years, they'd let me back in.

But some off-ramps aren't worth the toll, no matter the consequence.

Truth & Reconciliation

"Forgiving and being reconciled to our enemies or our loved ones is not about pretending that things are other than they are. It is not about patting one another on the back and turning a blind eye to the wrong. True reconciliation exposes the awfulness, the abuse, the hurt, the truth. It could even sometimes make things worse. It is a risky undertaking but, in the end, it is worthwhile, because in the end only an honest confrontation with reality can bring real healing. Superficial reconciliation can bring only superficial healing."

— Archbishop Desmond Tutu,
No Future Without Forgiveness

There were very few theological rituals and beliefs that, as a priest, I would have been willing to stand at-the-last defending. God's love for humanity; Jesus' sacrifice as ultimate love; the altar needing to become a table of real-life food; and confession as necessary for a people of faith. The problem a church or an individual Christian will discover (when they stop looking inwards towards their own shortfalls and deficits) is often the spawning of an anointed self-righteousness that too often gives licence to throw daggers at the rest of the world. There is a reason Jesus was so forceful in his teaching about forgiveness, and how you don't go after a speck in someone's eye when there's a two-by-four in your own.

I could not lead a Christian community that wasn't willing to name their own failings, as we tried to proclaim a prophetic vision of grace and mercy, and for some of the most marginalized people in our city. This is what I found in my final parish, though: a community that was one of the most vibrant and far-reaching of Anglican churches in Canada. It was a shocking magnification of what I discovered as a Canadian Anglican, so opposed to the language of sin. "Why does no one want to admit we've done anything wrong?" I would think to myself. How is it grace or mercy or *agape* or any other kind of love, if we're outright declaring we've earned our way in, and deserve everything we get—or can't even acknowledge the cross from where it all came? People didn't tend to like my posture on this topic. The leadership began having a fit. A junior priest on staff threatened to quit multiple times, and eventually had to be reassigned. The idea that we would ask anyone to look into their own darkness, so they might come to distinguish it from the light ... this was not a welcome surprise.

Like I've said, I was well medicated at this point. So, I just started ripping off band-aids everywhere. I made changes that should have been gradually introduced over a period of years, and I shook up the staff from Day One. My predecessor had made wide, sweeping changes himself, outside of church authority: doing away with the sacrament of Confirmation, affirmation of historic creeds and (outside of the dark days of the Lenten season) there was no need to confess anything. This place was incredibly well resourced; we served a hundred meals a day, five days a week, forty-four weeks a year, and spent more than $200K on the music programme. The deep social outreach made way for greater licence to spend money on the arts, and when I expressed my desire to make deeper ties into the gospel, well, the musicians would often suggest I'd win more points if I just preached about the music ... which worked! Sure. But not because they heard my message ... because it was a reflection of what they came to hear in the first place.

Unilaterally, I made the practice of corporate confession mandatory again in worship, because it should never have been removed in the first place. I hear how ridiculous I sound making a big deal of this, but I'm speaking in retrospect, and this is really how I felt. It wasn't a hobby horse, or a soap box, or a desire to make a point; I really did think this was at the core of what was failing in this church I found myself in. They thought the world should learn from them as an example, not from any holy wounds or words from another time or era, or any prophet or saviour who they didn't need. And to be fair, there was a small, strong, minority group of people who were hungry for good news from the pulpit. They just sat in the background so much of the time that I often forget how much strength I drew from them.

I've never been one to back down from a fight—and so I became quite zealous in my final year of ministry. I wanted everything I'd sacrificed to mean something *more*. I didn't sign up for this to become a community coordinator in a collar. I couldn't face leading this place and these people when among them it was so hard to find anyone who actually believed. Not in a bad way, mind you; these were lovely, charitable people, many of whom I came to adore. But don't talk to them about crosses or confessions or scriptures not performed. Music is just not something I ever worshiped, and if I did, it wouldn't be from the organ.

I picked a few key themes that swam against the stream and it wasn't long before I made some rapids. I wanted my stamp on this parish to be that we would learn to reluctantly speak a confession. *I've done wrong. I'm sorry. Please forgive me, neighbour and God.* I wanted them to learn what I thought I already knew: the arms of an extravagantly generous God. But there was so much historic trauma in this congregation—a congregation bound together because so many churches had sent them those who had been ostracized: LGBTQ folks, the divorced and remarried, clergy widows, ostracized clergy spouses, and rejects from across denominations. It was beautiful, how much coffee-hour looked much like the banquet table of the gospel stories, but many were genuinely offended if I connected that for them. It took me about a year to figure it out, with a little help from others, but it was a miracle that they were even in this building in the first place. I really started to learn something, when I started to listen while I was there. Not from the other clergy, or the staff or even the volunteers (who I liked to pump-up publicly but usually butted heads with behind the scenes), but mostly from the wounded in the pews that we'd rarely see at meetings or functions, outside of what Anglicans affectionately call "liturgy". I started to see how little you had to articulate your beliefs to someone who has been hurt by the Church; sometimes a broken spirit just needs a place to rest.

I completely burnt-out at the corner of Avenue and Bloor in Toronto. I lied to staff and parishioners and a close friend I was responsible for keeping boundaries with. I lied about my drug use, about my personal failings, and about my need to lay down my priesthood. I failed in my attempt to proclaim a faith I wasn't living anymore. I lost myself in a fog of deep spiritual unhealth.

***

I always felt like an impostor. Right from day one. I didn't lack confidence in either my instinctual gifts or my learned skills to perform the tasks of the job, but I knew full well that ninety percent of the people who'd ever known me would be flabbergasted at my career choice, or more precisely, that my career choice would choose me. At Fffie's wedding, when I was announced as a member of the wedding party, I was introduced as the brother who would have been voted, in high school, most likely *not* to become a priest.

The first time Heather ever saw me in my collar, the week before I was ordained, I stepped out of the bathroom and tip-toed into the living room, terrified of what I looked like. She couldn't stop laughing. She said it looked like Halloween, and she was right. It felt like a costume. I wanted to want it. I wanted to be the kind of man who deserved it. I wanted to not have hidden so much to get it and, maybe, then it would feel like less of a charade.

The year I was ordained to the priesthood, I was given the great privilege to preside at the nuptials of Sheldon and his beautiful bride. It was a surreal experience to play the role of the priest to family and friends who hadn't seen me since I was starting fights on Main Street. It was a redeeming moment, though; getting to show love for the big brother who'd stood by me. I was proud and honoured and humbled by the gift. I know it was grace, because I also know I didn't deserve it.

At the reception that evening, once everyone had their chance to kick back a few, and then maybe a few more, I began to be approached by old friends. Questions about my life, about the sermon, and if this thing I was doing was real. How did it all happen and what happened to *fight juice* and chugging beers out of the pool? Some conversations moved me in ways I still grapple with, and a few drew me right back into the heart of old shame. I was sober now—from alcohol—and maybe a little too proud. But I had wrestled with a lot of demons at this point, and I felt ready to face *the old me.*

Not long before I left, an old friend who I got into way too much trouble with as a teen approached me and pulled out the tab of my collar. He said, with a drunken stare, "I don't know how you've convinced all these people you're someone I know you are not. But don't kid yourself, I know you, and you do, too."

He wasn't the only one who thought so. I met Nadia Bolz-Weber at a homiletics festival in Denver. It was a quick five-minute connection after she'd given an inspirational address, distinguishing between confessing one's porn addition and casually mentioning you have to delete your internet history once a day. I told her how much I admired her vulnerability and her ability to speak so shamelessly and redemptively about all her own struggles and addictions and defects. She inquired as to why I didn't and was unsatisfied with my response. She didn't say a word for almost twenty seconds, and then in one sentence called both me and my faith shallow: "You really need to trust your people more." And she was right.

There were so many reasons why I didn't, though. There are real life consequences for exposing hard truths. But she *was* right, I'll admit it. I just didn't know who *my people* were, yet.

***

GiffontheWay Blog Post: August 2018.
Written, while running away, north of the 61ˢᵗ Parallel.

Secrets keep people sick.

It's one of those things you pick up in recovery. It doesn't really matter if it's addiction or mental health you are struggling with, or whether you find yourself well onto a path of restoration, eventually you face the deep and stark reality that secrets keep people sick.

I've had a lot of people question my practice of public transparency over the last number of months – struggling with how the discomfort that public admission of failure or brokenness makes them feel. To be fair, I have plenty of moments when I question it myself – who really wants to stand vulnerable in the public square – but then I remember that secrets keep people sick.

Secrets are what cause families to stay quiet about abuse, and trauma, and neglect. Secrets are how addicts force their loved ones to enable their behaviour. Secrets are how gossip poisons communities and relationships and toxifies the brain with deceit.

Failure we all have.

Darkness we all face.

Brokenness we cannot escape.

But secrets, we can defeat.

In one of the most torturous stories in scripture, Jesus encounters the Gerasene Demoniac, shackled and chained on the outside of town – away from the eyes of the community. Jesus frees the man thought to be possessed and irredeemable and sends any remnant of the demon into the abyss. The Garasenean people cannot believe their eyes. Jesus faced the darkness, embraced the marginalized, and shattered the chains that shackled this man on the outside of town. The people immediately beg Jesus to leave them, to get away from their home. They cannot face this kind of salvation for someone they had dismissed and sent out of their sight. They looked at him, they looked at what he had exposed, and then they took a long hard look at themselves. If he could expose this travesty, if he could call out this depth of darkness, what would he expose in them?

Revealing secrets doesn't have to lack discretion. It also doesn't require the sharing of every detail of our lives. But if I am to boast in my weakness and kneel at the cross, I must lay down my secrets bare.

Secrets do indeed keep people sick. But God knows even our deepest skeletons – and She offers us an abundant, redemptive and salvific love, shattering our shackles on the outside of town.

"Almighty God, unto whom all hearts be open, all desires known, and from whom no secretes are hid: cleanse the thoughts of our hearts by the inspiration of thy Holy Spirit, that we may perfectly love thee, and worthily magnify thy holy name: through Christ our Lord. Amen." – BCP (1662)

#Jesus #Salvation #Redemption

***

Eleven days after it was publicly announced I had been "defrocked" from my role as a priest, I boarded a plane back to Scotland. I could no longer avoid facing my mother. The demons and truth that had plagued me and kept me awake into treacherous hours of the night throughout my entire life, they needed to be addressed.

With the help of trusted friends; with bumps and many devastated tears along the way; without finishing with a nice tidy bow on a premature reconciliation; my mother and I faced the truth of our history. The trauma that became trauma that had retraumatized. Her failures as a mother. My failures as a son. The Church having failed us both. It was an important attempt at hearing each other. Two broken people who were children together in a small-town Scottish home –in the middle of a big Canadian city— finding a way to regain their empathy bond; to allow each other's heart to break for the other. Finding healing as a mother and as a son.

Boundaries

If you aren't a church person, this might not make as much sense to you (and if you are and it doesn't, you really need to look deeper into the life of your pastor or priest). Because, I promise you, across denominations, whether clergy want to be honest and open about this particular struggle or hide behind a genuine desire to live what they proclaim, they are struggling with it. Let me be clear: what clergy often struggle with is whether or not their relationships with individual members of their Christian communities are actual friendships in reality. From Day One, there is a power imbalance, which I learned—by my own fault, and devastatingly.

In my first parish, I learned my lesson, when I got into a political conflict with a parishioner in my living room; a man who believed Barack Obama had the *mark of the Beast*. So, in my second parish, I decided I would lay down the law from Day One. Heather was not required at any function or dinner invitation, and we didn't host parishioners in our home. This was my job, and I was going to set boundaries. I saw how failing to do this had destroyed leaders whom I'd admired in the past.

However, I will never be able to speak anything short of a word of love about this particular group. Kamalini O'Dunnigan and her husband Patrick practically gave their lives to this church while I was the pastor there for almost seven years. Wally and Olive Bedi, this ageless couple from India who were there from my first Sunday … people who were devoted, and sacrificial, and willing to face death and resurrection. The two dozen parishioners who made up both the parish council and the worshipping community when I arrived, were the most incredible people I've met during any season of my life. Ninety-five-year-old men born on an Easter Sunday at the close of World War I, or century-pushing women who'd been members since the founding priest carried them upon his shoulders in the early twentieth century. These people inspired me. They inspired the new neighbourhood that had changed over and around them during their hibernated death. They engaged the borough they were buried in with a new message of joy. At Christmas, they sang community carols, while handing out hot chocolate and candy canes. Creating an impromptu children pageant in the afternoon on Christmas Eve, a service that grew to have more children than we had costumes to provide. These are people who put their faith in giving away the stockpiles of what they had in resources, to serve the neighbourhood with free programming for children and, eventually, a Sunday dinner for anyone who wanted to belong and eat. We planted an evening community to meet the needs of people we didn't even know existed yet, and from what I see on social media today, they are leaps and bounds into a beautiful revealing of a kingdom we used to talk about.

Losing these people from my life was devastating. Most of them will never truly understand why. I kept ridiculous boundaries about family space and Heather's time, and where I was allowed to go and not have to wear my collar. But I was devastatingly in love with all of them; they took an impostor and made him a priest. In the end, one of the reasons I needed to move on was because I couldn't handle the dozens of intimate relationships that laid their burdens before the cross and, inadvertently, before me. Whatever I am now, I was certainly the priest to the people of the Church of the Transfiguration. My son was baptized in the same waters where I saw something incredible emerge from broken lives cared for, and nurtured, and renewed for life beyond our community. I blessed the relationship of a gay couple with the full support of the leadership. I saw broken lives welcomed without any requirement.

The words of a great twentieth-century preacher came to mind as I was writing this chapter, because the people of this church embodied the best of what I first heard him say, when I read it in school. "I believe in the possibility of a Christian world," Harry Fosdick exclaimed from his downtown Manhattan pulpit in the early twentieth century (hear him in context, please)— "not because I have been argued into it, but because I have seen Christian living done. I have seen it in persons firm as steel and beautiful as music, who poured out into this broken world a Christ-like integrity and humaneness which made spiritual life real. I have seen it in homes where what Jesus said ought to be the law of life was the actual principle of fellowship. It was not Christianity argued: it was Christianity achieved. I have seen it in social movements which leaped high barricades, belied the scoffing of cynics and the fears of friends, and opened the doors wide to new eras. It was not Christianity debated; it was Christianity done."

This is the place where I came to experience the most authentic revelation of what Jesus talked about as the kingdom of God, from top to bottom and on every floor. But I hated it by the end, because I couldn't really participate in it *and* be the priest who held the community together in the Eucharist. I built the extended family I had always wanted, and the Sunday dinner table with more seats than I could count, but it was never really going to be able to be a table where I could honestly sit.

I always had a small ministry team I trusted personally, and any of the designated churchwardens always shared in some social time with me. Information cracked when family meltdowns occurred but, for the most part, my personal life didn't belong to them, and they respected that deeply. My approach to priestly ministry was to compartmentalize my personal life for protection but, for someone like me, the permissible bifurcation doesn't stay bifurcated for long. I don't do well with keeping my own secrets, it seems.

When I arrived in my final parish, I met a social worker who put a lot of new ideas in my head. I'm not accusing him of manipulating me intentionally or claiming any misconduct here. His professional code of conduct is his and not mine. He sought to open up old wounds and vulnerabilities with me, during our one-on-one time when he was reporting to me each week. It was during a time I couldn't stop medicating, and he offered support and reassurance about it. He told me that I would become a better priest—and the only way I could be reachable to a group like this—was if I could be vulnerable and broken with them.

When shit started to go sideways, he was the first to say I had no boundaries.

I was at fault. I have never said I wasn't, but a narrative was quickly created, carved out and executed, while I was drugged out, melting down on social media. I'm not always certain exactly how far the narrative escaped me after I was ostracized (I have heard rumours and stories and lies) but I had little influence anymore. The anonymous emails that arrived in my inbox accusing me of rape and adultery and worse; they don't just delete.

***

Before I was ordained, I had no boundaries. There is just no other way to say it. I didn't give a shit for such a large chunk of my life before ordination; and I was also willing to just wear my heart on my sleeve.

The older sister of Rory's Uncle Donny's girlfriend (the one who I humiliated myself in front of before ending up in the bathtub, covered in puke) … well, the day prior, I sent her roses for Valentine's Day from a secret admirer. She was almost nineteen and I wasn't even sixteen yet. I got so drunk in front of her that I'm not even sure what I said. She was, quite literally, the prettiest girl I'd ever seen, and she actually paid attention to me. Even my ex-wife Heather turned me down the first few dozen times I asked her out. I met her while I was on a date with her roommate, and she wasn't having the-roommate-switch. I messaged, and called, and even showed up at her college residence to get her attention. We were practically engaged inside of a month. When I chose to step outside the trust and authority given to me by the Bishop and entered into an inappropriate relationship with someone who worked for me, I was far from considering boundaries or consequences anymore. In the end, I would be holding on to whatever I could, trying like hell not to lose it all. As I raise a young man—and wanting him to become better than his Dad—I will ensure he grows up knowing that overwhelming consent comes with respecting boundaries.

… But I am a boundary breaker. I have been my whole life. I can't keep to the rules for trying.

My golfing buddies will tell you (from an era when I could still afford it) I only played two ways: either we played by the rules and I enforced them ferociously, or I would take advantage and exploit every opportunity I could get. I won't say *cheat,* but if one guy is allowed to move a leaf off his ball, well I might give mine a kick. If one guy wants to take six-foot-gimmes, well, we'll just have to see. I was a rules Nazi, or Capone with a wedge. I've only ever had two speeds when it came to this.

There were eras when I cheated on tests without a single thought of conscience, and times I couldn't have done it if you paid me.

One thing is for sure: I *want* to break the rules. But I also want everyone to see.

***

Just after I was given notice I was being terminated, before I melted down publicly, between the meeting where I was told I was likely being 'defrocked' and the actual 'defrocking', it was a couple of weeks. I didn't call a lawyer right away or tell one of

85

Rory's uncles, or even his appointed godparents. I got in an Uber and had it drop me off at the airport with only the clothes I was wearing. I had a VISA card from the church, and I knew I had to be careful here. I was already being fired and accused of sexual misconduct; I did not need some kind of financial fraud on my rap sheet. But the treasurer and the churchwardens had told me multiple times that the points accumulated on the card were in my name and as far as they were concerned, they were mine. I booked a flight to Mexico from the terminal at the airport and boarded a flight two hours later. I didn't have a hotel booked or a contact there, and the last time I'd crossed the Mexican border was before I'd even known Heather.

There was this week in my life that was like no other. It was as though I stepped out of my skin and got to live in limbo for a short period of time. There was no need to give thought to reputation or consequence or expectations ... just me, before everything in my life would shift.

I met three lifelong friends from the neighbouring province of Quebec. They brought a dying soul back to life in six days. They danced with me in the moonlight and they swam with me until dawn. We dined together with new friends we met, and shared photos of our children and loved ones, and cried about trauma and betrayal. Vikki (who I could have fallen in love with if she'd have let me) told me I was a beautiful man. It struck me, only because I didn't remember the last time, I'd heard someone say that to me, or thought it would matter that they did. I was wild and unruly and beloved all at once. I did the air guitar at the beach club and Vikki kissed me in front of everyone on the beach. When I told them that I was a priest, they loved me even more. They thought I was crazy, and they never would have guessed ... but they knew we all play roles.

On one of my last nights in a little Mexican town, as the sun started to come up and the few of us who were still awake on the beach had smoked enough weed to keep us all tongue tied, someone got word of what I did for a living, and didn't know what to do with this information. I smiled, and said to them, "Love does not exist in the world. Prove me wrong!" A lively debate ensued. I told them about love, the way I'd come to know it, the way I knew darkness could never overcome.

Drunk off my ass, having done Jell-O shots off somebody's stomach in a little Mexican bar, I got high with a bunch of people on the beach, and as the sun rose, I told them about a guy named Jesus. It seems crazy to say it now, and I really don't mean it as some kind of strange evangelization. But I was as raw as I could be in that moment: my life was about to come apart at the seams. But still, I was a preacher.

> *"Judas could not face his shadow; Peter could.*
> *The latter befriended the impostor within; the former raged against him."*

> — *Brennan Manning,*
> *The Ragamuffin Gospel*

The Cross

*"You know, I'm 1,500 years old. I've killed twice as
many enemies as that. And every one of them would
have rather killed me, but none succeeded. I'm only
alive because fate wants me alive. Thanos is just the
latest of a long line of bastards, and he'll be the latest
to feel my vengeance – fate wills it so."*

–Thor of Asgard,
Avengers: Infinity War

There are times when I wish Jesus sounded more like the Norwegian
God of Thunder, willing to name his godliness and power in the
face of the greatest enemies he's ever known, with unwavering
confidence that he will never see defeat. But, contrary to whatever
Republican, evangelical, Americanized version of Jesus you might
have heard of or seen, the Jesus of the Gospels ends up hanging
dead from a tree.

Saint Paul says that the cross is foolishness to those who are
perishing, but to those who are being saved, it is the power of
God. But don't kid yourself: it is a treacherous means of violent
execution, utilized by one of the most brutal empires in history.

Jesus doesn't wield a mighty hammer or a sword or even a
shield. He submits to a humiliating and torturous death upon a
cross, on the edge of the Old City, for all eyes to see. While the
blood drained from his body, and his spirit left this world, he is

said to have forgiven his enemies—not just generally, but those who had just hammered nails into his hands and his feet.

Jesus of Nazareth was a first-century Middle Eastern Jew, a God who would give up his life for the people he loved, changing the very definition of "victory".

***

Rory was born in the midst of the historic Toronto ice storm. Heather was induced into labour because of a complication with preeclampsia and the induction didn't go very well. The monitors kept flashing on and off; hours passed by; generator power was shoddy; the elevators didn't work in the hospital and they began to transfer neonatal ICU patients to more secure locations. Heather was a warrior. No matter what she has ever succeeded or failed at, in any other situation in her life, she faced two days of excruciating pain, with substandard hospital care, and a genuine fear of what would happen next. She faced it down like a soldier in war.

When Rory got stuck in the birth canal, the doctor told me, before he told Heather, that we were headed for an emergency caesarean. I didn't really know what that meant in the moment. I just knew I had to agree, listen, and support my wife who could barely keep her eyes open.

I had to mask up, put a gown on, and wait outside of the operating room until they were ready. It was twenty of the longest minutes of my life, as I sat in scrubs wondering when I'd get to meet my son or daughter. When I was invited in, Heather had a curtain covering her entire body, and I sat down by her head. She was pretty out-of-it at this point and I smiled, trying to make her feel safe. All of a sudden, everything became clinical. The doctors removed the baby, and I didn't hear much of a scream, and so like they had instructed me, I made my way over to the warming station where he would be.

Rory was bright blue and not breathing and all of sudden, neither was I. "Is this real?" I thought to myself. "Is this some kind of bad dream? Is he going to die right here?"

I saw nurses and doctors rubbing his body, and one of them hit a giant pink button that I later learned was to call a *Code Pink*. I wasn't crying yet in this moment; in fact, I'm not sure I even moved an inch. I just stared at this little life that now belonged to us, and I didn't know if he'd ever breathe. I screamed at God in my head, "Whatever extra lives you've given me, asshole, you can take one of them and give it to him. You want a sacrifice? Take me, you feckless thug. He deserves a chance to live!"

I wonder now, if that's not exactly what Jesus was thinking from the cross when he gave up *his* life. I wonder how angry he was that he had to say it out loud to himself; when he had to face the treachery of their deceit. But there's a big difference between me and Jesus here. There's a *huge* distinction to be made about who we spoke these words for in each of our treacherous moments. Mine was for my little boy who is bone-of-my-bone and flesh-of-my-flesh, who I believe I am God-ordained to protect. Jesus spoke to the crowds, to the perpetrators, to the criminals and to the ostracized—regardless of their guilt—and said: "Take my life instead of theirs".

I couldn't breathe. I bargained with God. I offered my life for his. It was the most authentic moment I have ever survived ... the most painful moment of my life and the most life-giving. The day my son was born, the day I wasn't sure he'd live.

***

My first few days after being released from treatment in Nashville were a little different than what I imagine most people experience after being there. After a torrential downpour near the airport, my flight would be delayed two days on the back end. I made plenty of interesting friends while I was there, but rarely did we know of each other's actual identities. We didn't share names or jobs or details that would have given any secrets away, but we also shared so much more than we ever would with even our most trusted friends. It was a gift to be reminded that I was not alone in the adversity I struggled to overcome. One of the friends I made while I was there (unbeknownst to me) was a Grammy-nominated recording artist. When he heard my flight had been delayed, he invited me to stay with his family in their home for the weekend.

Jamie (we'll call him Jamie) and I had gotten close while we were at the ranch, and even started sharing some of our writing with each other. I didn't know what he did for a living, and he didn't know what I did back home. But we bonded over trying to express who we *really* were. He had lost a Dad before he even remembered knowing him, and I was trying not to lose my son. Once we arrived at his house, and realized we had a song brewing, he invited me to come with him to his studio to really write and record.

It took the three of us no more than a day, and we had written, produced and recorded a song that Rory now listens to almost every night before bed. It's not going Top 40 any time soon, and although Jamie rescues the recording by belting out the chorus, you've actually got me spitting out lyrics on the verses in a hip-hop ballad.

Stop laughing.

In the end, we fashioned a beautiful love song, from a father to his son.

<u>My Little Red King</u>

First one to hold ya'
Ain't never letting go
No matter where you at
I'm-a always be close
You the Luke to my Vader

You Simba, I'm Mufasa
That's the way God made ya'
And I think you're pretty awesome

Yeah Rory, Rory, heaven sent you for me
You're the S-on-my-chest;
    the best part of my story
You're the miracle I didn't know I needed
When I say it, I hope you know I mean it
You the Red King, my little Red King
(always gonna be)
You the Red King, my little Red King

Don't matter how tall
Don't matter how strong you get
I'm-a pick-you-up
Never let you fall
Never ever gonna love you less, and,
Life may change, and then change again
But one thing stays the same
It's me and you 'til the end

Yeah Rory, Rory, heaven sent you for me
You're the S-on-my-chest;
    the best part of my story
You're the miracle I didn't know I needed
When I say it, I hope you know I mean it
You the Red King, my little Red King
(always gonna be)
You the Red King, my little Red King

I love you, Rory. I'd give up my life for yours still.

***

From the foot of the cross, one of the gospel texts tells us that Jesus' mother stood, looking up at her tortured and dying son. She must have recalled memories of his infancy, his childhood, and his coming of age, as scattered images would have flashed across her traumatized brain. This woman, standing before the cross, had chosen to suffer for his very birth. Like any mother, she had repeatedly chosen his little life over hers. Having suspended her disbelief and listened to God's call, she had borne a son. This mother who had raised him on the back of faith, with love and compassion and duty, who had protected him from the evils of this world …. eventually she reached a day when it was time to let her child go out into the broken world.

But I imagine she thought: "How could *this* have happened? How could *this* be their story's end?" After everything good her son had given, this must have felt like much more than she was willing to give. As I re-read the story of Christ's torture and death from the gospel texts, through the lens of my next chapter of my life, I have been struck by the image of Mary, standing at the foot of the cross. From Good Friday to Opus Dei to Holy Cross in September—to the eucharistic meal itself— most of the Church across the globe and across denominations is *all about* celebrating *Christ's* sacrifice. But the more I enter into the story from new angles of economic circumstance and ostracizational struggle, I have found myself caught in reflection about *Mary's sacrifice* for Jesus.

The notion of sacrifice, in *our* culture, is one that we have learned to resist being drawn into. In this post-pandemic world of 2020, many of us have become increasingly aware how much we have conditioned ourselves to avoid being inconvenienced. We don't want to go without, and we want to believe we can have it all; *sacrifice* causes pain. Just like Mary, though, who stands at the foot of the cross, *all mothers choose sacrifice* as an expression of love, don't they? Throughout all pregnancies, in every generation, across the globe, mothers sacrifice health, comfort and their bodies, so that they might deliver life into this world. We tend not to think of it, with our modern medical assurances, but mothers also risk *their lives* by carrying their children to term. No matter the circumstance, and no matter the family, a mother's blood must be shed, and a mother's pain must be endured, for any child to be born. A mother's decision to give birth to life is to choose sacrifice as an expression of love.

I was five the first time I ever opened my eyes wide enough to see sacrifice. I remember sitting at the dinner table with my young immigrant family. My Dad had stayed late at work that night to make sure the bills were paid, and my Mum had prepared a meal for my sister and me. I remember looking at my mother's plate, in comparison to my sisters' and mine, and realizing that we had much larger portions than she did. Don't get me wrong: I didn't become aware that someone was going to starve, or that anyone was going entirely without, but from the eyes of my five-year-old self, I became deeply aware that my mother was choosing her children over herself.

As Jesus' mother grieved the sacrifice of her son; standing at the foot of the cross, it's hard not to think of what it would be like to gaze upon the destruction of one of our own children, right before our eyes. You might thrash and punch and strike to get near—risking everything you have—just to reach out and assure them that you are there. You might shout to them—offering yourself in their place; you might fall to your knees, not knowing what to do next. Aware of how much pain his mother had to be in, Jesus gazed back down upon Mary, we're told. The broken man on the cross gathered up all the energy he could from his tortured and bloody corpus, to offer his Mum comfort and care. Looking to his best friend who stood next to her, the old scriptures say he uttered, "Woman, behold your son." He knew his time was almost up, and his mother suffered the torture of his impending death. So, he looked to the family he'd made in adult life and, in brotherly love, entrusted her care to them.

One might ask how this could possibly be enough, since no substitute could ever replace a child. But from the height of the cross, God tells us that he can make family, even out of our own destruction. God will give us to one another, whenever there is need.

***

"All this pain
I wonder if I'll ever find my way
I wonder if my life could really change at all
All this earth
Could all that is lost ever be found
Could a garden come up from this ground at all
You make beautiful things
You make beautiful things out of the dust
You make beautiful things out of us"

–Michael Gungor,
Beautiful Things

It was the spring of 2019, when I still hadn't admitted to even some of my closest loved ones how bad it had all become in the deepest caverns of my brain; how little I was able to cope with or accomplish; how much pain I was still in. Sitting on a bench, at a busy Yonge Street intersection in Toronto—completely broke from trying to numb the pain; with tears streaming down my face—I could barely get a word out. I called my brother Donny, and I called my Mum. Don flew me to Calgary, and frankly, he saved my life. My Mum started sending money *every month* to pay my bills, money I knew she didn't really have to give.

Here's the undeniable reality I think I'll always have to face. The cross turns everything on its head, and straight up subverts the world. It's the thing I can't get past when I try and walk away. It is the only lens that reconciles *and* brings justice; it is the only road to healing *I've ever known.*

New Life

*"We used to grow priests in Ireland.
We used to grow them from bits of people that we
didn't like."*

—Tommy Tiernan

When you move houses as often as we did, growing up, you find yourself constantly starting again. Whether it's in a new school, or a new neighbourhood; new friends, new pressures, new ways of falling short. I was a freckle-faced authentic ginger kid from the motherland with parents who had funny accents. Needless to say, I got teased quite a little bit. But as I got older, I got really good at the fresh start, I could remake my image, my friendship circle. I actually started to *like* starting again. But at some point, you have to look backwards and integrate. You have to figure out what really mattered there, both *who* you really are—and *whose*.

Maybe others did this the summer after they graduated, or on a backpacking trip at another stage of life … maybe they walked the Camino de Santiago in Spain or found new depths of themselves in finishing a book. But that wasn't the case for me. I left the unexamined life behind when I was three. By the time I was in university I was already having a mid-life crisis. I had no real home to go to and feel genuinely safe. The Church adopted me and threw me a feast, every time I showed up. I felt secure in the motley crew of people I met, who always made so much freaking space for me. I believed I would celebrate Mass for the rest of my days, I really did. But the new life I found in the Church eventually did ask me to die to the rest.

At almost every stage of my life, I was told what to believe, what to hide, what to feel, what not to feel, and who I was supposed to be—often for the primary benefit and protection of the people who were supposed to protect and love me.

You don't get to make the Church your home when you're a priest, though. It's a hard matter of fact. No matter what you say about the Body of Christ or the Communion of Saints or simply referring to your congregation (as I did) as family. The priests are the stewards of the church, always meant to have a loose grasp on their belonging, because they have vowed to place the Gospel above their own and pass it along. Priests and Ministers and Pastors are not Mothers and Fathers of their communities – it's a bad analogy. They are people who have been sent to live and love a particular way in common life; and share their stories with us along the way. Through your priest, you are meant to see a reflection of the Gospel and, at some point, they were right: that was no longer me.

You don't have to be a carbon copy of Jesus, but how your life has been altered by encountering him … well, it matters to me. I might have been a good preacher and a solid pastor, but I was never a very good priest. I know the reasons why I'm not best suited to priestly ministry now, and if you've read this far, you know, too. But the hard truth and reality of it all is that the new life I found in belonging to the Church died with life in ordained ministry.

Good news, though … My faith says something really good happens on the other side of death. My faith says you have to spend a few days in a dark and hallow tomb after it all goes awry. But screw you if you stay there. Take your ball and go home if you think that's where you belong. Cause it sure as hell isn't where I'm building a house. I'll go elsewhere to build a home.

What I learned from my old *new life*? Here's a highlight reel.

I have to love Rory the way I need(ed) to be loved. I need him to know that he changed me; that phoning it in on our relationship would never have been good enough for me. I love him. Just as he is. Not as he will be or has been or will fail to become. Just him. I have to invite God—and for me it has to be God—to redeem any trauma I carry, by helping me not to inflict it upon anyone else. I must, at the very least, attempt to break any cycles that have spun. I have to make hard choices—sometimes to preserve and protect my loved ones—even the ones I have to limit time with, because I cannot always handle the memories that flood in. I either get busy living, or I get busy dying; that means I have to live as my authentic self. I have to discard shame and guilt for intentional choices and actions, accepting consequences and benefits. I have to put my need for lies on the altar of sacrifice, by living a transparent and open life. I must try to learn that fear doesn't have to be the dominating factor in my life.

It means I have to embrace my shadows and compromise a little bit with my demons, to the point that my son will likely know my failures well. But he'll never doubt I love him, I don't think. I pray he'll never have to wallow in any shame inherited, because I'm not carrying mine with me.

***

As the summer of 2019 began, almost one year after I left active ministry, I wasn't sure I was going to make it. I was still faking it as well as I could, trying to pretend it would all somehow turn out all right. As Bishop Cliff would say, I was anxiously awaiting my Aaron Sorkin finale. I was trying desperately to maintain as much visitation with Rory as possible and trying to have enough exciting moments so I wouldn't go jump off a cliff. I was living in a three hundred square foot bachelor apartment in the middle of the 'Six, and I was suffocating from the isolation.

In the early days of a summer we'd name from the syndicated sitcom, Seinfeld, calling it the Summer of George, my childhood friends and I began a summer to start again. Rory's uncles Rob, Donny and I grew up together in Markham and went to the same little Catholic elementary school. Donny's house was one of the few safe places I knew as a teenage kid: him and his two older brothers living in the basement, with shuffleboard and football helmets and ping pong. For a kid who grew up with an absent father, an overwhelmed mother and two sisters, it was a cool place to hang out.

The truth is, Rob and Donny dragged my ass out of the tomb that summer. They picked me up, put me on their shoulders and said, "They aren't keeping you in here!" My brothers came and found me and gave me my life back. They helped me remember who I've always been.

Summer of George Letter to Myself: August 2019

> My trip to visit Donny in Calgary at the Stampede was like stepping into the life I thought I wanted until I met Heather and I got ordained. It began a summer of deep, authentic conversations, opportunities to reflect, and love, and live into the raw care-free-spirit part of me that needs to let loose in the moment and not care what a single soul thinks sometimes. I described it to others afterwards –as did Donny boy– as being catalysts to one another to remember who we really are. It has been a similar experience for Rob as well. We now have a group text-thread that our childhood friends' message on regularly, helping each other give narration to our lives. It's a special thing when you have family who will love you no matter how bad you fuck up.

The thing I thought nobody ever liked about me; the witty creative writer, the intellectual thinker, the dramatist, the guy ripping-up-the-dancefloor and singing at the top of his lungs. But that's what they love about me, and it's what I'm finding new people I meet love about me too. It's just not what certain people want me to be.

It's so hard to write that and know it's true. I think the reason I've always identified so much with the LGBTQ community is because of how closeted I've been for so much –and in so much– of my life. No matter how much controlled vulnerability I shared on social media or in sermons, people tell me that most of my colleagues usually comment that no one really knew me.

I met a girl: Nikki. *It didn't last.* We actually met a decade ago at a conference through a mutual friend. She's a little eccentric and just the right amount of weird. She is stunning from any angle and in any light. We chatted here and there over the last month or so, and then over the last week we really started to connect. I have kept good boundaries, and we haven't slept together. But I feel really seen and heard by her, and she really fascinates me. I always have another question, wanting to get to know her better or in some way that makes me even more curious. The kiss we shared when I walked her home last night was better than any sex I've had during this last year. I haven't really experienced that before, or at least not in a very long time. I know I'm not ready for anything serious yet, and she's probably not the one. But she's someone I can imagine building a life with. It's nice to imagine that again. A future of my own.

I haven't said much about Rory, because those times are just generally great. I'm a little more tired when I have him, but I'm learning how to find rest and exercise for both of us when we need it. The two of us are finding a way to be together, as a family. I'm doing more things like reading him old chapter books I loved as a kid, *The Lion, The Witch & the Wardrobe*. I let him play more video games than I probably should, but his Uncle Rob comes over and he loves the same video games Rory does. Watching them together is actually one of my favourite things in my life right now. We went to the public pool the other day and I snapped a quick photo of the two them walking poolside. Looking at it afterwards was like looking at a very old and beautiful memory that was and still is, but one that might have been forgotten. Rory and I have figured out what it is to be father and son in this new reality that I wasn't really prepared for – and I'm going to work really hard at it.

I get to be whoever I want to be now, but I'm realizing all I really wanted was to remember who I always was. It's weird to know I have to grow back into that now, but in this *new old life* I've been graced with, I believe I will.

A New Kind of Man

"A Man who stands for nothing, will fall for anything."

—*Malcolm X*

I have to face my demons. There's no getting around it. This involves compromising with them at times, deep emotional and familial instability as well, and the exposure of some of my weakest vulnerabilities. However, I have to face them if I want a chance not to lose myself in the growing fog of clarity that comes with age. Not every day, not every hour, and especially not in the immediacy of life having fallen apart. But it mattered that I got up and looked in the mirror as much as I could over the last number of years, and still wanted to live my life, broken. It mattered that I remembered that there were people who loved me before I achieved a single thing. It mattered that I still had a life to live in love.

During my decade in ordained ministry, I prepared almost one hundred couples for marriage, and presided at each of their ceremonies. I participated in the burial service for more than two hundred beloved parishioners, helping families grieve the loss of a loved one. I baptized countless babies and adults, and counselled even more through their addictions, while so few knew the ways I was really struggling. I was always able to show just enough brokenness in my preaching so that others could relate, too. But I hid who I was as a man and as a human being. I proclaimed a message of hope from Day One, through to my last sermon. I shouted from the rooftops that no one was too far gone to receive the love of a God who would redeem them in the end. I still remember how moved I was, standing in St. Peter's Square, as the newly elected Bishop of Rome said, "It is we who tire of asking for forgiveness, not God who tires of offering it." But I hadn't forgiven myself enough to actually be able to *be myself* with others, because I'd have more to explain than I ever could. It took me twenty years of bad therapy before I found someone who I could actually be honest with; start to tell my authentic story. The amount of money thrown down the drain because I couldn't face the truth. It was a well-paid investment. Why? Because it got me here.

It's not enough to love *big*; you have to love *deep*. Surface love is easy. It's the kind of love Jesus made fun of at times. Like when he would preface a teaching, before dropping an epic "Love your enemies" rant, with an "even those guys love their family."

In a way, I really do have a new life as a new kind of man now.

I was formed from my childhood to be a priest. Most people don't understand this, or what it means. They know a priest or a pastor from some chapter in their lives, and think they know how they got there. They don't. My born-again ex-father-in-law was so rightly dissatisfied (from his Baptist point view) when, at his dinner table (while dating his daughter), I said, "I don't ever remember having a conversion experience, or being born-again – it sounds awfully painful— I knew Jesus when I was in the womb." He was fortunate if I didn't wink at him at the end of it. I was an arrogant little prick.

But when I got ordained, I felt the responsibly of the office, because I'd been prepared for it my whole life. This wasn't a career change or a shift in vocation, even though I had spent so much of my life screwing around. This is what my Mum had wanted for me; she formed me to be a priest. I had to leave my denomination and find another that might fit a sane enough approach; one that had a wide enough space to let me talk enough shit, and still allow me to get married and have kids, because celibacy sure wasn't going to work for any life I could imagine.

I no longer have a life *anything like* the life I would have had if I had never become a priest, and as many may attest to today, my life is no longer much like the life of a priest. The integration of these different lives has been a painful season in my life, and it has gone on far longer than I thought it would when I first began down this path. I have now come to accept a teaching that I forcefully tried to instil in others over the years: that the process of integration is an ongoing season and, if I'm intentional about it, and desirous of it, and I want to enter deeply into all four loves – *Eros, Philia, Storgē and Agapē* – I might just become the man I was meant to be.

***

The hardest confession I will ever have to make is the triggering affect my son has had on me. As much as I don't want to admit it, or ever have him know it, in his early years of life, when my symptoms got out of hand, frankly, he was a serious trigger. It's difficult for those who don't have traumatic stress injuries to understand how this could be—how my dearest loved one could also be a trigger of traumatic stress for me—but I will share my deepest and most shameful confession, to try and help others understand what those of us face, who suffer this way.

The thing nobody ever really tells you about addictive chemical pain medicators (Oxycodone, Fentanyl, Hydromorphone, etc.) is that they start by relieving the pressing pain of the moment (in my case broken bones), but it rarely ever ends there. As the weeks and months pass by, while you depend on those drugs, they increasingly start to offer pain relief for more than what they were prescribed for. All of a sudden, *other* pain doesn't hurt anymore. Emotional pain. Spiritual pain. Historical pain. Pain you didn't even know you remembered. It's gone. But then the prescriptions run out, and the broken bones may have healed, but every memory, every hurt, every abuse, every fracture of brokenness in your soul is all the more present and more menacing than they have ever been before.

As I mentioned early on, during my final year living with Heather, I struggled mightily with a drug problem. The high itself wasn't the problem (I'm actually pretty funny on Oxy). It was how the drugs made me feel when they stopped working. Then the wounds that had been covered with layers of bandages for years—sometimes decades—began to bleed.

Most addicts and alcoholics will be able to attest to this part; the first few hours of the day are absolutely the most horrendous. When I would open my eyes in the morning, all I could think was … how could I keep them shut? It is a treacherous time of the day for someone struggling with substance dependence, because it is usually the point when they have gone the longest without their substance. I didn't understand it at the time, because I was just trying to survive, but from the moment Rory woke up and started making the beautiful noises of a little child, and his mother would work to get him fed and ready for school, well … I couldn't move. For hours sometimes. I stayed locked in my room and I hid under the covers. It wasn't that I didn't love him, or even her … I didn't understand what was happening. My brain felt so much shame, and guilt and self-loathing, and genuine, overwhelming pain.

It caused me practical problems at work, because I was always late for meetings and commitments, and I couldn't get anywhere on time. I phoned-in my relationship with my son for at least a year; I really wasn't very nice. All I cared about was the pain *I was in*, and what it would take to get out of it. I felt like I was stuck in my childhood home again; with no options, no escape, and the walls closing in.

It's true: I didn't feel safe at home growing up, but I did have safe places.

When I was a teenage kid in Markham, I spent as much time as I could in Rory's Uncle Donny's basement. Three teenage boys living in the bottom half of their family bungalow and, when you passed the threshold of the stairwell, you knew they ruled this roost. There was freedom here; to say the wrong thing, to dress the wrong way, to relax and unwind, and occasionally wake up to a handful of shaving cream in the face. I learned a tonne, both good and *less good,* while I was there. When Chip wasn't home, I would take his spot any night on the bottom of the bunk bed. When shit would go sideways at home and I no longer felt safe, I'd often run with a full-on sprint to Donny's house and stay in the Seaver basement. No one ever forced me to explain why or how or when I was going home; we usually just ordered pizza and watched the game.

In the fall of 2019, when I wasn't sure what home would ever look like again, Donny decided to become Rory's uncle. He moved home from Calgary, took a job in Toronto, and agreed to live with me. People joke about it being an episode of Full House, with Donny playing Uncle Jesse, Rob as Uncle Joey, and me as Danny Tanner. The analogy is not a perfect fit but, with Donny's help, and with memories from our shared past, in *this chapter* of our lives, we have built a home that is safe. There is no pretence or posturing here. We are honest about our struggles and we make space for the ways we know we can't meet up.

We live in brotherly love, three men and a Rory.

The giant wall leading up the stairs to our rooftop in our home has taken on a special meaning. Upon it are my university degrees, as well as Uncle Donny's, and Rory's Kindergarten diploma, signed by his teacher and principal. There are plax-mounted articles from my life in ministry, and photos from when I was a football coach. There are pictures of Rory's early accomplishments; his first perfect spelling test in grade one, and his sportsmanship award at soccer camp. Donny's football trophies are mounted high for something to aspire to; and in the corner where you might not even notice it, are a chalice and paten with which I used to celebrate the Eucharist.

I brought Rory home this last year, and no matter how long we live here, I've learned to build a home where I can breathe.

***

I am not my father's son. I think that's clear now. I tried like hell to be my mother's ... until I crashed and burned. I'm no longer Heather's husband or the golden boy priest – but I am still Rory's father, and an Uncle and a brother, and a cherished friend, and a man in need of forgiveness and reconciliation. I have been a success and a failure. A sinner and a saint. A confessor and one deeply in need of confession.

Most of all, as I look back on my history, with an eye for what's next, I know, wholeheartedly and without reservation, that I am broken, fractured ... *and beloved*. When I look in the mirror, I now know what it is to be known, loved, and seen, as me.

It took a while, but Jesus' words held true. My name is David and I have been redeemed.

Epilogue

Today is December 12th, 2020. It has now been two years since I was *deprived of ministry*. I have sought to appeal the decision to the Diocesan Court of Appeal in the Ecclesiastical Province of Ontario, on medical grounds. I have been denied a hearing. Short of bankrupting myself with legal fees in pursuit of a small moral victory, I have made the decision to relent. On this day, on whatever holy ground I stand, I relinquish ordained ministry in the Anglican Church of Canada.

I am no longer a *defrocked* priest.

There is an Orwellian episode in the cult classic TV series of my youth, Star Trek: The Next Generation. Captain Picard has been captured by the Cardassians, and is being tortured and investigated for information. Before they physically abuse him, they show him four lights and ask him how many lights he sees. He answers, "There are four lights," even though they beat him unless he will admit there is five. Darkness, question, answer, beating. It was as tragic and unfathomable a situation as a little suburban preteen would likely ever have to consider. When he was rescued—when his body had been broken, but his spirit continued to refuse to relent—he admitted to his rescue company that, even though he'd refused to say it to his torturers, by the end, he really thought there might be five lights there.

So, if that's it. If I've laid my orders down, and asked God the grace to let me go … if I am no longer defrocked or deprived or excommunicated (yet) or a priest, who am I to the Church today? Who am I to this Jesus guy I kept talking about? Well, grace for me isn't picking back up the stole or elevating the Eucharist anymore.

It's not being given a charge to pastorally care for a community. Grace has invited me to leave one of the greatest privileges in my life, as a season that is now complete, and still embrace the faith of my baptism that led me to become a priest. It is absurd to think I won't ever step into a pulpit again or crack open the scriptures for others to hear what those crazy prophets have to say next. But I am relinquishing ministry as a priest.

Corpus Christi (Ecclesiastical Latin), Ubuntu (Zulu), Shalom (Hebrew).

The Body of Christ, I am bound in your humanity,
may we live in peace.

It does mean I'm taking away the Bishop's right to licence me. I offer myself to the Church, uncollared and without filter now. Who needs Father David? You've got me.

***

To my family. I imagine that it isn't easy to be a family member of mine, but frankly, it wasn't always picnicking and rainbows being a member of yours either. I've done my very best to portray each of you honestly –and with charity— acknowledging the systemic failures that were beyond each of us. If I didn't tell the best stories about you, I also didn't tell the worst. I take responsibility for the places I fell short in your lives, and I am sorry for the ways I have failed you when you needed me most. I am grateful for any redeeming moments we might find together again.

To those of you who feel you have been harmed by the chaos I've ever caused, in whatever chapter of my life you ended up caught up with me, here's the thing: *Most of you really wanted to be there.* Don't kid yourself: the ride is often exciting. There's a reason I've never been short of "friends". Some of you offered me power and authority and the keys to the kingdom, knowing full well it was a terrible idea for me. I am sorry for how anyone has ever been hurt by my actions –especially those who were without fault— but let me be clear one last time, I've rarely ever caused chaos all by myself.

For what it's worth, in the end, *this* is what I believe.

GiffontheWay Blog Post: May 2018.
Written from the floor of Rory's bedroom.

The core message of the Gospel is about how God cleans the crap off us, and then invites us to clean the crap off each other.

After preaching this essential message on Sunday about what Love (agape) looks like to God, I got a bit of a terrifying reminder tonight. Having come home from a lovely date night with Heather, I peeked my head into Rory's room to give him a kiss and whisper goodnight. As I lay down next to him, I quickly realized that he'd been quite sick – everywhere – in his sleep. All over his sheets, his pillows, his pajamas – I felt like I was elbows deep in the mud. I picked him up and yelled for Heather, as he became startled and a bit confused. I took off his PJ's and wrapped him in a blanket, while Heather stripped the sheets off his bed. He cried and moaned and yelled about feeling so ill, asking me to make it go away. I felt helpless and heartbroken and even a little scared (knowing full well that we all get sick from time to time). He had puke in his hair, a little on his cheek, and his breath was downright revolting. But I didn't think twice about kissing him, or holding him close, or getting it smeared all over myself – I just wanted him to know it would all be okay. Then for half a second, he calmed down, looked up at me to say, "I love you, Daddy." And then he threw up on me.

I wonder if that's not how God finds us, so often. Tired and sick, yelling and screaming, covered in all our own crap and mess. And yet She looks at us, She holds us close – never afraid of all our muck that will smear and spread. She hears both our cries for help and lament, and our moments of returned affection, and probably even knows what's coming next.

Agape love. The very heart of the Gospel. God made manifest in the mess.

#Fatherhood #Jesus #Agape

"Oft hope is born when all is forlorn. *The world is indeed full of peril, and in it there are many dark places; but still there is much that is fair, and though in all lands love is now mingled with grief, it grows perhaps the greater.*"

— J.R.R. Tolkien

Afterword

It's all a matter of perspective, I guess. From my side, at that point in life… the glass was half full. 25 years later, and I lived most of the stories you just read. I promise you, from my lens they look different. Does it take away from their validity: No. It does mean a different image is captured from each lens, and perhaps the story is different too.

As I read the memoir for the first time, I was drawn to it. I couldn't wait to read each page and see which of his childhood memories would pop up next. As I was taking it in, I wrote down questions I wanted to ask him, and inevitably, a familiar one arose; the question I asked during my self-proclaimed *epic best man's speech*, "Do you know who you are?"

Dave's parents were angels in my eyes.

His mother provided me with clothes in high school, from a clothing store that I could never afford. She and I had meaningful discussions about God and spirituality; she introduced me to the poem, *Footprints*. It was her way of showing me there was a higher power watching over all of us. When I was finished my post-secondary course, she gave me the cost of my tuition, so I might have a chance at life without starting off in the hole. As I grew older, I realized that she struggled with her own issues, but as a teenage boy who came from a broken home and struggled financially, she wore a set wings through my lens.

Dave's father was a friend and confidant. He worked hard to provide his family with everything he did not have in Scotland. I admired his tenacity and quick wit. He challenged me to reach my potential and taught me life lessons. At two separate points in my life, he helped me secure places to live. The apartment 403 with Dave in our senior year, and the white house where I rented a beautiful home for a ridiculously discounted rate. I can honestly say that without his support I would not be where I am today.

Dave's Mum & Dad provided me with things I needed as a teenager and as a young adult. It is not that my parents were not good parents; it's just that it takes a village, as they say. To reverse the roles, if Dave read my memoir, he'd likely remember different stories of my own mother and father and the influences, he has told me, they had on him.

After I put the draft down, I had to reflect on the words I read and the emotion they stirred. Dave has had an addictive personality his whole life. There has often been no in-between. When he falls in love, he falls hard and fast. When he drank, he drank to get drunk, and often found himself visiting the island of liquid courage. When he preached, he put his heart and soul into it, trying to inspire and enlighten everyone who would listen. Driving past the "off ramps" is the perfect analogy. He continues to live this way today – with a conscious effort to slow down and tap the brake a little more often.

As I read the final chapter, *A New Kind of Man*, it appears now more than ever, Dave has taken hard steps to admit his faults, live for the moment, and set himself up for tomorrow. I don't know if we ever *know who we are* but living to be a good father and an honest man who admits his faults and tries again – it's a damn good step in the right direction.

Sheldon
Professional Firefighter.
Big brother to many more than he knows.

116

Acknowledgments

To my Mum & Dad:
For what it's worth, I love you. I think about you both every day.
I grieve what we've lost. I am grateful for what I've found. Rory
loves you both more deeply than either of you know.

To Heather:
We made the most beautiful boy together. He has an amazing Mom.

To Rory's uncles:
You are my ambassadors of Quan.

To my sisters:
You deserved a better big brother than me.
You are both stronger women than most people will ever know.

To my editors: Martha Barnard-Rae & Murray Watson.
Thank you for pushing me, believing in me, and having the
audacity to tell me when I'm wrong.

To RG, CBR, AL MR & anymore that come:
You are made in the image and likeness of both your parents. Take
what is good. Challenge what isn't. Learn to love what is broken inside
of you, because one day, it will be your greatest source of strength.
Don't forget who you are or who you come from: Alba gu bràth!

To all the teachers that told me I'd never amount to nothing...
(MDHS Parking Lot)
Okay. I'm done. Peace.

Appendix

Resources worth reading
(that inspired RT)

Anything and everything by J.R.R. Tolkien, C.S. Lewis, J.K. Rowling, Aaron Sorkin, Malcolm Gladwell, and *anything you hear of in the future* by Douglas O'Dea or Robert Crocco.

Alighieri, Dante. *The Divine Comedy: The Inferno, the Purgatorio and the Paradiso.* Translated by John Ciardi. New York: Oxford University Press, 1985.

Bolz-Weber, Nadia. *Shameless: A Sexual Reformation.* New York: Convergent Books / PenguinRandomHouse, 2019.

Burke Harris, Nadine. *The Deepest Well: Healing the Long-Term Effects of Childhood Adversity.* Boston: Houghton Mifflin Harcourt, 2018.

Evans, Rachel Held. *Searching for Sunday: Loving, Leaving and Finding the Church.* Nashville, TN: Thomas Nelson, 2015.

Fosdick, Harry Emerson. *A Preaching Ministry: Twenty-One Sermons Preached by Harry Emerson Fosdick at the First Presbyterian Church in the City of New York, 1918-1925.* Edited by David Pultz. New York: The Church, 2000.

Machiavelli, Niccolò. *The Prince: On the Art of Power.* Toronto: Duncan Baird Publishers, 2009.

Manning, Brennan. *The Ragamuffin Gospel: Good News for the Bedraggled, Beat-Up, and Burnt Out.* Portland, OR: Multnomah, 1990

The Book of Common Prayer, issued by Thomas Cranmer in 1662; available online as a PDF at: https://www.anglican.ca/wp-content/uploads/BCP.pdf

Tutu, Desmond. *No Future without Forgiveness.* New York: Image Books / Doubleday Religion, 2000.

Tutu, Desmond. *God Has a Dream: A Vision of Hope for our Time.* New York: Image Books / Doubleday Religion, 2004.

Tzu, Sun. *The Art of War.* Translated by Samuel Griffith. London: Oxford University Press, 1971.

X, Malcolm. *The Autobiography of Malcolm X, As Told To Alex Haley.* New York: Ballantine Books, 1973.

"I refuse to be a role model
I set goals, take control, drink out my own bottles
I make mistakes but learn from every one
And when it's said and done
I bet this brother be a better one
If I upset you don't stress never forget
That God isn't finished with me yet"

— *Tupac Amaru Shakur*

Printed in Great Britain
by Amazon

49047346R00078